L·A·U·R·E·N·C·E

Olivier

MELVYN BRAGG

LAURENCE

Olivier

ST. MARTIN'S PRESS/NEW YORK

For Ian McKellen

Picture research by Chris Haydon

Design by Craig Dodd

Library of Congress Cataloging in Publication Data

Bragg, Melvyn, 1939—
    Laurence Olivier.

    1. Olivier, Laurence, 1907-   . 2. Actors—
Great Britain—Biography.   I. Title.
PN2598.O55B72   1985   792′.028′0924 [B]   85-2675
ISBN 0-312-47523-3

First published in Great Britain by Hutchinson & Co. Ltd.

First U.S. Edition

10 9 8 7 6 5 4 3 2 1

Previous pages: The film *Hamlet,*
1948

CONTENTS

ACKNOWLEDGEMENTS

The author and publishers would like to thank the following for providing photographs and illustrations:

Colour (listed in page sequence)
between pages 48 and 49 Kobal Collection, with the exception of Garrick Club/e.t. archive (Garrick Club portrait) and National Film Archive (as Henry V)
between pages 128 and 129 Granada Television (as King Lear); Kobal Collection (in *Marathon Man* (top photograph), *Sleuth* (bottom photograph), *Love Among the Ruins*, *Clash of the Titans*); National Film Archive (in *Lady Caroline Lamb*, *Marathon Man* (bottom photograph), *Sleuth* (top photograph)); TV Times (in *Brideshead Revisited*, *A Voyage Round My Father*)

Black and white (listed alphabetically)
Academy of Motion Picture Arts & Sciences pages 41 *bottom right*, 54 *top*, 112 *top*
All Saints 23 *bottom right*
BBC Hulton Picture Library 33 *right*, 34, 36 *bottom*, 41 *top left*, 80, 88 *top*, 90 *bottom*, 116, 121, 131
Birmingham Repertory Theatre 27 *top right*
Craig Dodd 35, 36 *top*, 37
Zoe Dominic 16 *bottom right*, 128, 129, 130 *bottom*, 132, 133, 138
Douglas Fairbanks jnr. 64/65 *bottom left*
Fox Photos 69 *bottom*
Friedman-Abeles 111, 123
Granada Television 137
Gryspeerdt 130 *top*
John Vickers Archives 16 *top right*, 17 *top left*, 31, 76 *right*, 81 *top* and *bottom right*, 89, 90 *top*, 91, 92, 93, 94, 95, 126 *top right*
Kobal Collection 17 *bottom*, 30 *middle right* and *bottom right*, 43 *bottom*, 51, 54 *bottom*, 55 *bottom*, 59, 60 *top*, 63, 66, 69 *top left*, 74, 79, 86 *top*, 87 *bottom*, 88 *bottom*, 97 *bottom*, 98, 99, 101 *top right*, 102 *bottom*, 108, 122 *top*, 134, 139
London Weekend Television 26, 140, 142, 143
Mander & Mitchenson 30 *left*, 44 *right*, 45, 56
Pierre Manevy 115
Angus McBean 17 *top right*, 53, 57, 72, 73, 103 *bottom*, 106, 107, 112 *bottom*, 113, 119 *top*, 126 *top left* and *bottom*, 127
Don McCullin 70, 71
National Film Archive 24, 27 *bottom right*, 38, 55 *top*, 58, 61, 76 *left*, 82, 87 *top*, 96, 97 *top*, 100/101 *left*, 101 *bottom right*, 102 *top*, 103 *top*, 104, 105, 119 *bottom*, 122 *bottom*
New York Public Library, Lincoln Center 44 *left*, 50 *right*, 62
Lord Olivier 2/3, 11, 14, 16 *top left*, 18, 20, 21, 22, 27 *top* and *bottom left*, 28, 30 *top right*, 33 *left*, 41 *top right* and *bottom left*, 43 *top*, 47, 50 *left*, 64 *top*, 65 *right*, 69 *top right*, 78, 81 *bottom left*, 85, 86 *bottom*
Molly Thomas 23 *top left*
John Timbers 16 *bottom left*, 124, 125
Talli Wyler 60 *bottom*

Every effort has been made to trace copyright holders of the photographs used in this book but author and publisher apologize if they have unwittingly infringed copyright.

INTRODUCTION

When you first meet Laurence Olivier you feel that you are encountering a pageant. You have seen him rearing high on his white horse, sword unsheathed, urging on England as Henry V. You have been drawn to his icy, at-odds quality amid the athletic antics in the *Spartacus* epic. In a school party you saw *Hamlet*, and were chastened. In *Rebecca* he assumed the restless, upper-class poise which seemed to personify elegance, and in *Wuthering Heights* he somehow made that fantastical male monster, hero of the Moors, into a credible Heathcliff. He has been Restoration man, Marathon man, Suburban man, the Ambassador, the Fop, the Evil Kingly Genius, the Drunk, the Smutty Comic. Your imagination is infested with a Dickensian population of characters, faces, expressions, gestures, roles, moments of piercing awareness. The man you meet, always courteous in a pleasant, old-fashioned way, has a face very like the thousand faces you see every day in a city street. He is a clean slate, almost a blank.

The contrast between this ordinariness, this anonymous private face, and the powerful variety of public masks never ceases to impress and bewilder you. It is as if, having seen the pageant in all its gold and plumage, it disappears when you come upon it, dissolving itself into the mundane figure of an average-sized man in an average-looking suit giving you the perfectly normal time of day, softly shaking hands and shattering all illusions. Which, of course, he intends to do: this private mask is also deliberate. That is to say, the 'private' mask he assumes at first for someone like myself – a stranger, with a request. I wanted to make a portrait of Olivier for television. I knew he had been very ill and was still not well (this was 1981). I knew he was hauling himself back into circulation by the lifeline of an autobiography. I knew that he was very wary of publicity especially in the country of his birth (he had, after all, appeared in advertisements on American television, advertisements which were never to be shown in England). I arranged to see him in my office.

The reason for this was simple. The only way in which I could persuade him to come in with us and spend the time necessary to make a decent portrait was to show him what we intended to do. We had made up a reel of clips from some of his most memorable roles on film and television; we had copied up some newsreel material; we had sorted out some photographs; we had already prepared a list of the people, places, locations which would feature in the film. He came along, tired-looking, even sad in his stooped bearing, whispering that yes, he would appreciate a cup of tea and no, he preferred a hard chair thank you. We ran the reel. It lasted about two hours.

At first he commented a little – always to exclaim about another actor – 'Oh, that's old . . .', 'Dear me, it's . . .', 'And look at . . . isn't she marvellous'. Never emphatic, these comments; perhaps wistful. Then there was silence. His roles fled by on the screen before him in ten-minute segments. He was sitting a yard or so in front of me and so I could not see his face. The screen images looked out at the old and ill man sitting in the hard chair. He had told me – and I believed him – that he had seen scarcely any of these films since the day they were finished. Here he was, fifty years ago, forty, thirty, twenty years ago – wonderfully handsome, now full of power, now astonishingly bold, now bitten into a furious inner passion. As the silence thickened, I felt that I could not have done anything more tactless. Here was someone who had exhausted himself in a massive fight against cancer, who had said he would never have the 'guts' to go onto the stage – his indisputable great love – ever again in his life, who must have known – he who knew his own face and look so profoundly well – that he appeared no more than a wisp of the man he had been: and what had I done but thrown in that face the clearest possible proofs of his former, past, irretrievable greatness. I wanted to apologize, to pull the plug on the relentless reel which pushed out image after extraordinary image at this man – grey-haired, in a dandruffed striped suit, intent and immobile before the glorious passage of his many lives.

Finally, thank God, it was over. I was almost choking with embarrassment. Olivier did not turn round and I said nothing.

When he did turn round his eyes were red from weeping. He had not made a sound. He reached out and took my hand. 'OK, old boy,' he said. 'Let's give it a go.'

I kept notes over the next eighteen months. I saw films, television plays, stage adaptations, newsreels, archive footage, publicity material from the studios, out-takes. There were interviews with Sir Ralph Richardson, Sir John Gielgud, Dame Peggy Ashcroft, John Osborne and dozens of others who had known and worked with him, most especially, of course, Joan Plowright (Lady Olivier). The early draft of his autobiography was read, as were some of the many books, reviews, appreciations and reports of a man who seemed to have enjoyed at least five major careers. Finally there were the photographs, hundreds of them.

There is, I believe, a profound sense in which the look of Olivier describes the man: or rather, in which the many looks, faces, masks reveal the many men he is. An album such as this, then, can have one simple function: it can provide a catalogue of the characters created by a great actor compulsively driven to versatility, seeing his task and his art to be rooted in making himself different every time he assumed another part. The words which accompany it can best be introduced by way of negatives.

This is not a biography. The best and fullest biography I have read is John Cottrell's *Laurence Olivier*: it is amply detailed and set beside Olivier's own equally full *Confessions of an Actor* gives a substantial helping of information about how he can be recorded from the outside and how he feels he wants to present himself from within. Nor can I carry the authority of those who worked long and closely with him – Sybil Thorndike, for example, Noel Coward, Tyrone Guthrie, Terence Rattigan, John Osborne, Kenneth Tynan. They knew him intimately and have often spoken and written acutely, in Tynan's case dazzlingly, about him. And there has been a long line of critics. Ivor Brown, James Agate, Richard Findlater, Bernard Levin, W. A. Darlington, Harold Hobson, Irving Wardle, Michael Billington et al. are observers whose descriptions of his many particular performances often read as well as anything they have written. Olivier's genius seems to have spurred them on. There is no sense in which I can attempt to match that compendium of regular, industrious criticism. This is an essay. It comes out of a fascination with the man and an attempt to understand him.

Whenever I met Olivier – after that initiation in my office – I met him armed to ask questions. Together with the production team – Bob Bee, Nick Evans, Jill Freeman, Jenny King, Gabriel Clare-Hunt and Chris Haydon, who also organized the photographs for this book – I prepared myself as thoroughly as possible. Not just because that is normal practice. An extra concentration and anxiety came into it because we were filming over a long period during which Olivier was prone to sudden relapses and intent, with much of his greedily harboured energy, on writing his autobiography. The result was that both parties were directing their attention to the same object – Olivier's life-work; consequently he may have been readier to answer since his own preoccupation evidently dovetailed with our ambition. He wanted to organize his life for print: we wanted to portray it in film.

One of the advantages of doing a public interview with any artist about his work – the source and routes of which are often resolutely private – is that, once the invitation to take part in the interview has been accepted, there are the obligations of courtesy and 'public face' which promote honest responses. Curious though it may seem, I have often been able to hold more intimate, more detailed and more fruitful conversations with an artist – about his or her work – in public than in private. Privacy allows the elisions of shorthand and the loopholes of ambiguity. Put an artist in a public spot such as television and a sense of occasion, of decency, of playing straight, of not being caught out by the inevitable claque of friends and enemies severally gathered around their screens, generally prevails. Television is a good lie detector and sensitive people know it.

Olivier, of course, is ten thousand times accomplished as a man on the public podium, in the eye of a storm of publicity, at the centre of a furore, followed and haloed, as most of his professional life has been, by lights. That was a problem. Would he be merely on parade for us as well? We took our cameras to him time and again over those eighteen months. Even when we met for a meal or a resumé there would be notes taken. He came to trust us, I think. He said so, and was most generous in his appreciation of the final product. But perhaps he tricked all of us all of the time. Certainly some of the television critics were swift to point out that Olivier was 'acting the interviewee'. To which one could only reply, 'But of course.' Of course. The interesting questions are: why was he acting, who was he acting and how much of the Olivier we were concerned with was more truthfully revealed by this acting?

We were all in the game within the first ten minutes of the first morning's shooting. He had just been finishing his autobiography and was full of the pains of authorship. He reclined on a sofa, needing to keep his left leg up because of the danger of clotting; nevertheless it was a grand, authorial pose with a shelf of books just peeping into the right of frame. He wore a fawn, leather-buttoned cardigan of a type I vaguely remembered being sported by Simenon, and one or two of the better-regarded English writers of the forties. His spectacles were firmly fastened to his nose although all he had to look at was me, four or five feet away, and all he had to avoid was the camera, six or seven feet away. Avoid! But it was the pipe that did it. The pipe was a little too heavy for the teeth, that was the trouble, and a touch temperamental, or was it that its smoker was no great pipeman? 'A good prop, you see,' he acknowledged, a couple of seconds before the thought articulated itself in our minds. 'All authors smoke pipes, don't they?' And the tease was on.

In one sense it never stopped. I never expected it to. This was the game he played to tell this sort of truth: the truth about himself as he was prepared to admit it. Meanwhile, though, there were the off-camera times, the observation of the process whereby Olivier could 'touch' so accurately and often so delicately on people he had been – the boy, the youth, the matinée idol, the film star, the bureaucrat – and the parts he had played. Because we filmed on several occasions we found him mellow, we found him merry, we found him tetchy, brusque, even angry; we found him morose, sentimental, abstracted. So was he always cunning?

I think not. I think that he might well have taken for his motto this couplet from Congreve's *The Double Dealer*:

No mask like open truth to cover lies

As to go naked is the best disguise.

The more I thought about it, the more I saw the thousands of feet of rushes and yards and yards of celluloid of others talking about him, of him in role after role, flickering from youth to age, from gorgeous princeliness to plain weariness across those small screens in the film cutting rooms, the more I came to believe that

couplet from *The Double Dealer* very useful; it is when he is in disguise that he is naked. He is telling the truth about himself all the time, whatever role he plays.

He himself has insisted on this, bluntly, with an unostentatious shrug of words, on many occasions. 'The only time I ever feel really alive is when I am acting,' he has said, in many variations. And as to the purpose of acting, he has been equally firm. 'There are many dimensions in the art of acting,' he said when speaking to some drama students, 'but *none* of them are good or interesting unless they are invested with the appearance or complete illusion of the truth.' When not acting he has consistently described himself as 'bored' or 'boring', with 'no point of view': he once said 'without acting I would die, I suppose'. 'People would never believe how very *ordinary* he is at home,' Joan Plowright has said. Acting himself as the writer/interviewee, then, was his only method of telling us all he could bear to tell us about the work and life on which we questioned him. For at the time of being interviewed he was indeed a writer and a distinguished elder statesman of the theatre looking back on a life of achievement: we got some truth in that.

This truth presumes that we believe what he says and take it for granted that he believes it too. I have found that many highly complex artists are prepared to describe themselves in simple terms and abide by the description. I believe Olivier when he says that the only time he ever feels really alive is when he is acting: I believe that when he is not acting one part or another he is bored, very 'ordinary', even a cipher. I think the extraordinary thing about Olivier is that, in whatever role, he is always telling the 'open truth', always 'going naked', and also always 'in disguise'. That *is* the real self.

I have declared the modesty of my credentials compared with a considerable number of others who have written about Olivier – and indeed, as the man said, there is a great deal to be modest about. Let me now balance this with a conceit. The essay is divided into five parts, preceded by a prologue, followed by an epilogue. In nothing else but that can I imitate and pay tribute to the writer whose creatures have most certainly hoisted Olivier to greatness. Each part – or shall we let loose all restraint and release a coven of hostages to fortune? – each Act includes a description of a place in which I met and interviewed Olivier over the period I spent with him. The hope is to let first-hand reporting rub words with the reflections of Olivier himself, the observations of others and my own attempt at understanding. The photographs are essential to this piece: by his looks ye shall know him.

When he became a peer – the first actor to be raised to the peerage – Olivier, who still prefers 'Sir' to 'Lord', dug up his family motto. *Sicut Oliva Virent Laetor in Aede Dei*: 'I rejoice in the House of the Lord, even as the olive tree flourishes.' Faith and Nature were kin.

It is a remarkably accurate comment on his life and work.

PROLOGUE

It is a truism that we are different people to different people. A woman can assume the roles of wife, mother, daughter, lover, careerist, friend, intimate, acquaintance, enemy, zealot, nag, refuge, and she will be the same basic person but each time reveal a different aspect of herself. It is a truism also that many of us want to be different people. A man might want to be a famous writer, or a spy, a political hero, a hermit, a scholar, a soldier, a scoundrel, an Olympic athlete, a decent family man, a Beat. However impossible the ambition, the wish can be nonetheless keen.

When we are children, both these truisms seem true. When children play games, they do not bother to pretend to be the characters they are assuming, they adopt them wholesale, they swallow them in a gulp. 'I'm Robin Hood – you be Will Scarlet.' 'I'm Luke Skywalker – you're Darth Vader.' 'I'm a nurse.' 'I'm a mother – he's the baby.' 'I'm Spiderman – she's Wonderwoman.' I am. You are. We are. No qualifications. The impression of any strong character makes a complete imprint on a child and out comes the small self-declared clone. Children seem to have no trouble at all in 'being' other people: it is entirely a pleasure and apparently both effortless and natural.

Aging brings limitations. Childhood's easy access to a multiplicity of possible lives narrows to a track or two – the routes or ruts we have to follow. Most of us realize, too late, that we have but one life, that much of it has already been determined and that most of it is now spoken for. The full realization of that terrible restriction is like the clamping on of an iron mask. All those sensual dreams of potential, of possibility, of variety, of alternatives – all are expelled from the riveted face of reality. The game is up.

Yet it will not lie down. And it is those who create characters – writers, film makers, comedians, newspapers sometimes, and actors perhaps most of all – who keep it active. They provide the inspiration for the expiring body of our imaginative needs. We are sucked into their novels, their movies, their media-invented lives and, most surely of all, we are most willingly seduced out of ourselves by actors. They play the parts we once could so easily have reached. They live out the many lives we know we could and should have enjoyed. They tell us what we are not, which is so often what we want to be. They are all the futures we will never have. And when one man – such as Olivier – portrays in himself alone so royal a flush of possibilities then we are moved not only to admiration but also to curiosity. Not – how does he do it, so much as – how does he dare do it?

For in some low throb of memory, we can dimly call up the times when we too could 'be' multitudes: we turned our backs on those multitudes, thinking that less was more, that to specialize was not only inevitable it was mature, not only sensible but profitable. Yet in Olivier we are faced with a man who retained his multitudinous existence and is also mature, has profited, has proved that more is more. How has he held onto that easy childish boldness? Where did he get the nerve to sweat out the imperatives of 'growing up', 'settling down', 'setting your sights', 'specializing', 'stop dreaming', 'stick at one thing'?

Look at the photographs of Olivier. He wants to be everybody. He uses every bit of skill and private sorcery to convince himself and us that he is anybody he wants to be. And he is. A blood-blinded Greek; a spinsterish, old, country justice; a crippled, malicious, envenomed King; a modest young naval officer; a swarthy, vain, wild, jealous Moor; a gallant; a tinselled prince; an oh-so-very-English-county squire; a fashionable husband; a wild, romantic lover; a London clubman; a drunken failure; a conservative with nothing but the preservation of kippers on the Brighton Belle to occupy his mind; an old, wild, tragic and mad-demented King; an administrator. He has brought so many lives

into him and discharged them as his own. We press our faces against that in admiration and envy like Victorian street urchins pressing their noses against the panes of richly furnished shop windows.

And this allows him to be the heroes we want to be but never, quite, manage: he is the villains we dread being and sometimes, almost, succeed at. He can let his courage storm the stage and his cowardice palpitate in the spotlight. He can be the most ecstatic lover and the impotent. He can use all the reaches of his many selves and summon up those embryos of other lives we have crushed on our way to the security of singleness.

Not that this singleness does not bring its own rewards and compensations: and it is undoubtedly true that some of the best and most valuable work done is accomplished by people of fierce, limited dedication. But there are all the other glories of those unused, unknown lives, all inside us, forever unable to get out. As if we were a hive of bees and only one, or at the most two, were allowed to pass into the outer world, the rest condemned to a perpetual buzzing in the frustrated dark. Those who create characters – on the page, on celluloid or on the stage – and most strikingly those who inhabit other characters, tell us what we want, perhaps what we need, to know: that we are various, that we are not one but many.

That Olivier has done this over a vast range of characters and decades is undeniable. His many roles, even in close-up camera shots, record what? A master of disguise? Of make-up? Of camera-spooking trickery? He is the same man, yet he can appear so different. As we all can. But his differences and his different appearances are on such a scale, cover such a range as to leave our commonplace manoeuvrings from role to role as no more than the fumblings of a beginner. The different people in him are loosed on the world in full war paint. And the disguise, the make-up, all the artifice, are little more than gestures. The real change is deep within Olivier himself: for it is different parts of himself he reaches for as the demands of the many characters rise up to meet him. It is himself he lays on the line. His own heroism; his own cynicism; his own villainy; his own fury; his own tenderness. 'There must have been something of Archie in me all along,' he said of Archie Rice – 'The Entertainer'. 'It's what I might so easily have become.' So with all the others. Olivier, like all supreme actors – and authors in many forms – is driven by the relentless compulsion to let out this whole Pandora's box of different people, characteristics, virtues, vices, strengths, weaknesses, that beset him and demand to be released. When he is not opening the cage door to let prowl one of his beasts, he is not 'dead behind those eyes': what we are allowed to see is the wary gaze of fear. In all his many costumes, behind all the false noses and the wads of make-up, under the wigs and beards and padding and armour, he is telling us the truth about himself. He is always himself, always naked.

Top row: The film *Hamlet*; as
Mr Puff in *The Critic*, 1945; *Oedipus*,
1945; *Macbeth*, 1955; *bottom row:* In
Rhinoceros, 1960; in *A Flea in Her
Ear*, 1967; in *Marathon Man*, 1976

17

EARLY DAYS

The first day's shooting had been rearranged a couple of times. He was not quite as well as he wanted to be. He needed another week or two on his autobiography. When he did arrive he was both effusively and convincingly apologetic. We set up the cameras in the upstairs room of his comfortable country cottage-house. There was a warm, early summer sun. He pottered about and settled himself comfortably – the left leg had a tendency to swell up rather painfully, needed to be kept up, underpinned by a cushion or two. That pipe was produced with a nod and a flourish. While the lighting men coped with the sun's dazzle through the windows, Olivier and I chatted a little, deliberately off the subject. Yes, he had finished the first draft of his auto-biography. It was far too long. He had discovered how extra-ordinarily boring he was. It had been the hardest thing he had done but he had done it and by himself. Yes indeed, it could be called useful for this filmed interview: he was all up to date with himself, too full of himself you might say, absolutely primed. And deter-mined, he said, given the rules I had laid out for the interviews (no liberties to be taken with private matters; no holds barred on the parts and the other public work), to be as truthful as he possibly could be. It was as easy and pleasant a set-up as I had ever enjoyed. The sun, the man, the calm, the time to shoot. 'Action!'

It is useful sometimes to begin with a vague and general question, more of a net than a line, a friendly heave up, more of a handshake than a lead. On the whole, I asked, looking back on his childhood, what was his strongest overall impression? And into that serene room, from the world-famous actor in his mid-seventies who wanted to make up to us and wanted to be truthful, came the unhesitating response. 'I was frightened. More than anything else, I was terrified.' It was chilling.

For more than two centuries, the men in the Olivier family elected, predominantly, for the Church. Olivier's father was the tenth child of a parson and after an early (quickly squashed) hope of being trained for opera, a foray into dramatics, a short sharp lesson in financial and academic failure, he became a school-master and a cricketer of county standard; then, well married, well set up with his own private school and a life of Edwardian privilege, he gave it all up, in his zeal for God, unplugged himself from material contentment and took his family along the strait and frugal round of bare pickings and Anglo-Catholicism.

Laurence was the third child: there was a sister six years older and a brother about three years older. Laurence's sister has quite straightforwardly confirmed his vivid recollections of being 'frightened'. It appears that their father could not stand his youngest son, could not tolerate him. Perhaps he was associated with a bitter convulsion within the marriage, or with the very indifferent worldly luck that came to the Oliviers after the dramatic entry into High-Churchmanship, or maybe there was, even at that tender age, rivalry. For certainly it appears that his mother Agnes absolutely adored him. He made her laugh, she

Top: Gerard Kerr Olivier

Above: Agnes Louis Olivier (née Crookenden)

Top: Sybille

Above: Dickie

Birth

Name Lawrence Kew Riviere

Date Wednesday. May 22nd 1907
at 5 a.m.

Birthplace 26. Wachen Road. Barking

Weight first weeks 7 lb.

Exercise

First took up from the floor
& stood alone (a safe) Aug 29 1908 Aged 15 mths

First crawled 13 Months Old.

First walked

had hair so long she could sit on it, she was brown and quick as a gypsy, he has repeatedly said how much he adored her and how no photograph can show off her beauty. Perhaps this imp at the feast provoked jealousy in the breast of the father. It has been known. His manner, though, or his revenge, was to frighten the boy who would remember it and possibly use it for life.

It was all the more frightening because Gerard Olivier was the priest of God. To be despised, rebuked and condemned by father on earth meant, sure as eggs were eggs, that the Heavenly Father too thought you a very poor specimen. And Olivier's religiosity was early intense. There was 'Laurence's Shrine' where solitary private services were conducted by the five-year-old arrayed in a popish eiderdown. He was very vulnerable to what he could intimate as the desires of the Almighty. By the age of seven he was inside the altar rails, an acolyte to his own father-Father, terrified even more by the fear that he might do something 'wrong', misdirect the wine, forget which response came after the blessing of the bread, just think one wrong thought and the Might of the Lord would descend on him. This fearfulness is the molten core of his childhood.

Agnes his mother was bedrock. She seems to have loved him particularly: even now he talks of her with an unaffected girlish spooning. It was she who – consciously or not – took him out of the spheres of his father. She preferred a better class of church to the one her husband preached in and attended the fashionable All Saints in Margaret Street, central London. It had a famous choir school and she placed her elder son, Dickie, there and in 1915 – at the third time of trying – slipped in the scraggy little Larry. It was a sanctuary.

For five years he boarded there, lived a life of the monastery, sang solo to expensively dressed, connoisseur congregations, took part in the religious dramas of Anglo-Catholicism, blotted up great scores of choral music, great periods of Jacobean prose, great rituals in glittering vestments. Like Richardson and Gielgud at about the same age, he longed to be a priest.

We went back to All Saints one afternoon after a rather hedonistically heathen lunch at Overton's. Not knowing what to offer a man such as Olivier, I suggested oysters and champagne to start with which, although he was 'not to drink much, dear boy, not today nor any day', he diffidently accepted. A couple of bottles later he was in fine form directing the driver up and down the back-street mazes of central London as we weaved about looking first for All Saints and then for a parking space. Finally we got out and walked: he, though an hour or two ago declaring himself 'rather low', and indeed then looking it, by now transformed and as jaunty as a sailor on leave.

Inside the church he was instantly subdued in tone but at first the bubbly style would have its say – 'the most beautiful church', 'look at the Lady Chapel – over there', 'most wonderful acoustics in London – you aimed for the West wall – there – and up it went

To Larry
From Mother.
Jan 14.
1915.

into the ceiling', 'marvellous organ', 'here's where we used to process – I was a boat boy, carrying the incense'. Soon it wore off and either tiredness or too pressing a rush of memory gradually blocked out talk. He simply sat and looked about him.

For this was where it all started, he said. Anything that mattered to him. He had been 'too weak a vessel' to go into the priesthood and he was not now a practising Christian although he kept his own faith, but here he learnt, he knew that you had to dedicate your life to a great purpose and with passionate conviction.

And inside the choir school that great purpose was plain. For next to God, the All Saints choir school worshipped the theatre. Geoffrey Heald, a teacher at the school, put on productions with such panache that it became the thing for some of the greatest actors of the day – Ellen Terry, Forbes Robertson, the young Sybil Thorndike – to go to the performances. Olivier seems to have been an instant star. His doubting father was one day greatly flattered to hear his son praised in the very highest terms by one of the very greatest actors in the land. Shrewd Ellen Terry saw his potential at once. As did Father Heald – whose tiny (fourteen-strong) school turned out at least three renowned actors – who commented of Olivier's Kate in *The Taming of the Shrew* that it was the best he had ever seen. A comment complemented by W. A. Darlington, who reviewed the fledgling production in the *Daily Telegraph* and was only one of several

Above: Ellen Terry, an early admirer

Right: The Duke of Newcastle's annual outing for the All Saints Choir School to Selsey Bill, 1917 (Olivier front row left, his brother Dickie front row, second from right)

national theatre critics present: he praised Olivier roundly and concluded, 'I cannot remember any actress in the part who looked better.' The performance was put on at Stratford-on-Avon in Shakespeare's birthday week and the fourteen-year-old Laurence carried the wreath in the procession from the theatre to Shakespeare's grave.

When you look at Olivier as Kate the Shrew you meet a strange expression. It looks not vulnerable but hurt and powder-ready to retaliate. The attitude of the face and the body are womanly rather than girlish: there is little skittishness in the look of this Kate. She seems drawn not from youth but from the world of older women. A world just then cut off from him by his mother's death.

Olivier has described how utterly bereft he felt.

He is also prepared to appraise the strengths such an acute loss might have given him. Not that this serves as compensation or consolation: but something came of it. In the Olivier household of genteel poverty where a chicken could be so finely sliced it could serve the family for three days, where the bathwater was shared by the three males and suits were passed down from better-off uncles, nothing was to be wasted. Or perhaps Olivier, wanting his mother's early death to stand for something more than a tragic loss, cannot bear to let her go without claiming for her one last gift. Her death might have given him, he says, that quality of detachment, that haunted quality.

Or it might, in its way, more brutally, have killed off some central root of affection so decisively that he has found nothing to replace it since: only relief in the taking on of roles. I have always found it most odd that he speaks of his attraction to Joan Plowright – his third wife – in terms of her 'likeness' to his mother: that in this younger woman he found at last or reclaimed the tie broken when he was thirteen. He was over fifty then. I accept that he is speaking the truth as he finds it. What, then, of the time between, when his character, his career, his achievements, his fame, his whole complex trajectory of life was established and so richly developed? At the very least this confession of rediscovering his mother in Joan Plowright must point to that mother having been 'lost' or repressed for an immense haul of his life. As he has declared his mother to be at the root and centre of his affection and capacity for affection, perhaps her death created an empty centre, devastating the young boy the more cruelly as he was at full stretch. And to appease that empty centre, to keep himself company or to staunch the loneliness, he turned to others: but not people. Roles.

For which people could he turn to? He was already an outsider. At thirteen a 'star', a solo boy, a pet of the famous and a name in the newspapers, he was about to be catapulted into the unknown and inhospitable territory of an English public school which he hated. They thought he was a cissy; they thought he was a show-off; they thought he was a lousy sportsman. They were right, he

Above: Dressing up

says, one – two – and three. 'I tried to be anonymous,' he recalls. 'All I wanted was to be like the rest.' He is convinced that he would have succeeded but for the other pull: acting. 'They had heard about the acting.' He was Puck in the school play. National reviews once again and yet Olivier is convinced that his success only filled his school colleagues with disgust.

Puck had been a release but the boy wanted to disappear into the crowd. When his elder brother Dickie set off for India for the first half of his nine-year stint, Olivier, with his father in the bathroom that night, asked when he could follow him into the Indian Civil Service. The few years at public school had unravelled all the embroidered dreams woven from the rituals and sermons of his father, the excitements and triumphs organized by Father Heald, the feeling of a wonderful, chosen life to be lived inspired by his 'darling mother' and his intense espousal of a personal God. The Civil Service was now the answer. From the pinnacle of being adored, applauded, singled out and encouraged to feel that the world could be commanded by his ambition, he had plummeted to a view of himself which insisted that he be 'like everyone else' and, to make doubly sure, as like his steady, reliable elder brother as possible.

It was here – as Olivier has often told it – that his father abruptly told him not to be silly, he was to be an actor. Olivier was not only delighted with this directive, which rekindled hopes he had held since his last years at the choir school, he was, just as importantly, 'amazed that Father had taken the trouble to think about me and to make a plan for me'. It is a peculiar scene. Naked widower priest and spindly teenage son in cold bathroom in Pimlico playing out a love scene. For it is in that tone of voice that Olivier still now refers to it. His father – the awesome, frightening, terrible Gerard with God on his shoulder – had received his son. In some way, Olivier must have felt himself blessed.

His father set out the terms and conditions for his career and, in his gratitude for the affection so long withheld and the release from the fear so long endured, Olivier obeyed them to the item and may be said to have abided by them since. There was a Miss Elsie Fogerty, his father said, who ran the Central School of Speech Training and Dramatic Art: Laurence was to go there, get a scholarship and further, win the £50 bursary which was on offer. Without it his father would not be able to support him and there would be no acting career. From the very first, then, at the age of seventeen, Olivier was plainly told and knew he had to believe that success was entirely up to him and that earning money was part of it: what he wanted had to be earned and in cash. Any ideals, any vows on the cross of dramatic art, any swearing by the sword of aestheticism was as foreign to this enterprise as clean bathwater.

He did exactly as his father ordered.

If his mother's death had scooped the heart out of him, thus, as

Left: Elsie Fogerty

it were, fancifully speaking, leaving the space free for so many other characters to inhabit and comfort, his father's mundane battle plan sent him spinning into his career like a top and like a top he whirled his way through Miss Fogerty's school of five boys and eighty girls.

Miss Fogerty seems to have been a matriarch of talent. She warned the young man about his brow ('a weakness' – eyebrows too thick, hairline too low) pointed him away from over-gesticulation and put him through the hoops of voice training, dancing, learning different parts, acting.

Peggy Ashcroft, an exact contemporary with whom he shared the top prize – she Portia, he Shylock – described him, mildly, as 'uncouth'. He looks at that time positively in from the Bush. His hair sprouts out of scalp and eyebrows; his complexion is almost swarthy; his teeth are splayed and gappy; his nose seems not so much dominating as overwhelming; his suits, we are told, were short at the sleeve and equally ill-fitting at every other point; his diet was buns, buns and coffee and not many buns and his energy, according to Peggy Ashcroft, was 'quite tremendous'. She laughs at the recollection: even now a little appalled at the violence of it.

But he had to move fast: his mother's place had to be filled and

Opposite: The young Olivier. As Richard Coaker in *The Farmer's Wife*, 1926, aged 19; Birmingham Repertory, aged 19; becoming a matinée idol in his early twenties, foreshadowing his performance as Heathcliff in *Wuthering Heights*, aged 32

Richard Goolden
in "The Farmer's Wife"
1936

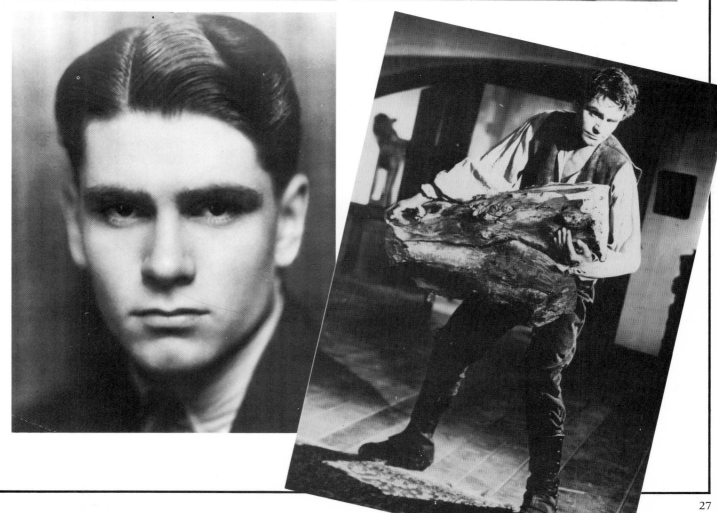

his father's enabling imperative meant that he had to succeed. If he failed to succeed he would be landed with himself, his empty anonymous self. He needed all those other people: all those people who could neither frighten him nor die on him. And all those people he could love. Love and be. He has often said that one of the key tips in his life was Tyrone Guthrie's injunction that unless he 'loved' the character he was playing then he would never play it fully. And another tip he took firmly on board was 'all parts are character parts'. He wanted to get hold of those characters to express himself: without them he would simply be himself and that state always has and still does puzzle, bore and dull him. 'I never know what to think or say. I never know what to do.' Characters were his spokesmen.

Olivier can still execute a brilliantly mimicked memory of his early failures, malnutrition, falling flat on his face at his first entrance onto the professional stage and several firings for various crimes of unprofessionalism, most usually giggling on stage. In our interview he castigated himself at this period as 'a twerp' and laid into his twenty-year-old self so robustly that one or two critics thought he was just enjoying the knockabout. Not, apparently, so. There is much evidence of his twerpiness, of his vulgarity: wanting to rip down the backcloth on stage (during performance) because he knew 'the girls' were changing behind it and he fancied seeing 'all those bare bottoms'; calling the company which gave him his first real start playing in halls and swimming baths in the suburbs 'The Lavatory Players'; being rescued and repaired by those old friends of the family and soon to be his own 'dearest friends', Lewis Casson and Sybil Thorndike. He seems to have whirled about like a dervish, terrified to be out of work, almost hysterical when he was in work – but work he must.

He was fortunate to go to Birmingham in 1927 – still only twenty – to join the company of Barry Jackson, who employed and often discovered and 'brought on' an astonishing number of the finest actors and actresses. Birmingham gave him exactly what he needed: work and characters. In a year he played about a dozen roles and, as we can see from the photographs of Tony Lumpkin and Uncle Vanya, he was already – and the virile roughness of those early attempts is very touching – straining to do what became his life-plan: never to look the same twice. He will refer to this rather musingly, almost, even, reverentially, as a 'compulsive quest for versatility', or he will dismiss it as 'a childish desire to show off so that people coming into Birmingham one week would say, ''Oh! That *can't*, surely not, be the very same young man we saw looking so very different last week.'''" Whatever mood he is in he never baulks at referring to it. And in it, he found his release and his equilibrium. From now on that was to be his life. Work, new characters to absorb, new parts of himself to display through the inventions of others. Whenever he was not working, whenever he was without a 'character', he

Below: As Tony Lumpkin in *She Stoops to Conquer*, aged 20

would declare himself null and void. The only way he could be himself was to consume others.

For the title role in Tennyson's *Harold* he learnt at least 3000 lines in one week. His devotion to detail was already evident. Everything, he confessed openly, was to be used. Everything he saw, overheard, encountered, heard of, was to be used. No one was safe. He prides himself on storing away information which he can conjure up years later when he needs it. For example, when we spoke that sunny morning in the Sussex cottage which he has cunningly and appropriately made look like a mini Elizabethan residence, he told – alas at too great a length for our film – an anecdote of Shandean-shaggy-dog-story complication about a dinner he had à trois with Charlie Chaplin and Paulette Goddard. All the time he was speaking I wanted to say 'Please cut, please get there', or I was thinking 'How will it edit? What can we do with this except show it at full length but there is so little time and so much other more directly germane material.' On and on went this anecdote as Olivier amused himself – he knew, once he had become labyrinthine by accident that the wittiest course was to stay labyrinthine by design – but the point was this: Chaplin and Paulette Goddard were having a row in front of Olivier. The burden of Chaplin's complaint was not – oh no! – that Goddard had taken a fancy to another man, but that she should provoke a row in front of a guest. In his 'funny American cockney,' Olivier said, 'impossible to imitate,' he added – and then imitated it – 'Charlie kept saying that her behaviour was "an insult to my mind".'

'You see,' Olivier said, 'it wasn't enough for him that he was the funniest clown in the world; he wanted to be thought of as an intellectual. Well, I used that, eighteen years later, when I did Othello. In the first speech to the Senate, Othello speaking as one intellectual to another. You know?' Olivier smiled angelically and then either to mitigate the confession of stealing from a private conversation or of retailing the private conversation itself, he punctured his own observation instantly. 'Got a laugh,' he said. 'If you can find a laugh or two in Othello, it's very helpful.' Just the sort of anti-intellectual remark he likes to specialize in.

He stole from other actors, particularly the screen stars. At this time Olivier was swept into the general passion for matinée idols – Ronald Colman, Douglas Fairbanks. The glamour! The elegance! The style! The dash! The moustache. 'I said to him' – Ralph Richardson recalled the time when they had just met – 'I said, "What's that?" "That's my moustache," he said. "What do you want that for?" I said.' He never told Richardson that in his first flight of enthusiasm for *the* moustache he had been so impatient that he had *painted* it on. Nor would he have been likely to confess to the man who was going to become his lifelong friend, colleague, advisor and sparring partner, that he had virtually redesigned himself.

Sparring with Richardson. *Top right: 21 Days*, 1937 (USA title: *21 Days Together*); *middle right: The Divorce of Lady X*, 1938; *bottom right: Q Planes*, 1937 (USA title: *Clouds Over Europe*); *opposite top left: Arms and the Man*, 1944; *top right: The Critic*, 1945; *bottom: Richard III* on stage, 1944

"BEES ON THE BOAT-DECK"
(AND IN THE BONNET)

He had shaved back and plucked the hairline, at last taking notice of Miss Fogerty's comment on his 'weakness' (low fore-head). His eyebrows were plucked. He took exercise to fill out the barely nourished 'wires' as he called his limbs. He dressed gaily. He went to nightclubs. He met the girl – Jill Esmond – who was going to be 'my very first wife'. He was going to be Beau Geste.

The transformation is somewhere between comic and worrying in its neat, sweet all-completeness. The rough gypsy boy with a face full of bumpkin mischief and unpredictable energy has been wiped out. Even the glowering intentness of the many roles at Birmingham have slipped quietly away into the wings. Stage front, tailored like a swell, glistening with the very latest line in handsome maleness, he presented his new self – Beau Olivier.

The Beau Geste role was to be translated onto the stage and, like every young actor in England, Olivier was after it. It is impossible to believe, looking at private and stage photographs of him at that time, that he could have been made for any other role. Ronald Colman released him into the twirling twenties. The moustache and later its memory gave him what Richardson called 'his cool: his panache'. Beau Geste was to bring him what he most wanted aged twenty-two: all the fame in the world.

He was by no means the leading contender and, refashion, reshave, remodel himself as he would, it seemed for some time that he was scarcely a contender at all.

He took a lead part in a play by R. C. Sheriff called *Journey's End*. It ran for a few weeks and, as was becoming usual, the young Olivier was picked out with some excellent notices. The cast believed in it with great conviction and when it failed to find a backer all of them stood by it – all that is, except Olivier. The author thought that Olivier had been rather reluctant to play the part of the young First World War officer – Stanhope – who takes to whisky to stave off cowardice. He was right: Olivier left to play Beau Geste at the irresistible salary of £30 a week.

Beau Geste, full of sound and fury, full of effects and acrobatics and the sight of money being burnt, flopped. *Journey's End* reopened to nineteen curtain calls, a run of 600 performances, world-wide success, a film and fortunes for all involved.

In the next eight months, while *Journey's End* clocked up audiences, money, prestige, records and excitement to become one of the phenomena of the theatre, Olivier played alongside it in several London theatres: in the New Theatre as Prince Po in *The Circle of Chalk* – a flop; in the Lyric as Richard Parish in *Paris Bound* – which flopped; in the Garrick as John Hardy in *The Stranger Within*; in the Fortune as Jerry Warrender in *The Last Enemy*; in the Arts as Ralph in *After All* – flop, flop, flop. He went over to New York to play Hugh Bromilow in *Murder on the Second Floor*. Flop. He maintains that not doing *Journey's End* – the big hit - was one of the best pieces of professional luck he was ever to enjoy. That, anyway, is his story and he sticks to it.

His reasoning makes sound retrospective sense. While Colin Clive, the new Stanhope, had one time to shine, Olivier was constantly being re-presented to West End First Night audiences and critics who would generally find something kind or admiring to say about his performance while being lukewarm or worse about the play. And – again in retrospect – being stuck as

Right: In *Beau Geste* on stage, 1929

Below: With Lillian Harvey in *Temporary Widow* (his first film), 1930

Stanhope, Stanhope on stage, Stanhope in New York, Stanhope on celluloid, could have meant Stanhope for ever: nearly the contemporary equivalent of getting typecast in a television soap-opera. On the other hand . . . there are those who said he was more than a bit fed up. And after all, he had created the part in the first place.

Help, though, was at hand. If not the US Cavalry then Noel Coward. The darling and idol of the boulevard, lyricist, librettist, writer of comedies, actor of wit, and no mean tap dancer. He had written *Private Lives*, which he knew would be a smash hit, for Gertie Lawrence and himself. (Himself also directed, of course.) There were two other parts, neither up to much. The husband was fundamentally dull, a lump, a feed, in all conscience little more than a device. He wanted Larry in the play 'because I said I must have somebody who's physically very attractive otherwise Amanda would never have married him. He must have something to give, he hasn't got much in the dialogue way. And poor Larry never really enjoyed playing it much. I think he enjoyed acting it with me, we had great fun, and curiously enough it did him a lot of good.'

It gave him £50 a week and enabled him to get married to Jill Esmond, a young, very successful actress from a theatrical family

Below: Marriage to Jill Esmond, 1930

whose outspoken views on marriage ('If ever the man I married behaved decently towards me or I towards him only because it was laid down in an unwritten marriage contract, I should feel it was high time we parted') added another charge to a glittering theatrical wedding – Ralph Richardson, Jack Hawkins, Nora Swinburne – graced by aristocratic gifts including a necklace of pearls from Princess Marie-Louise who loved the theatre, and held in Olivier's beloved All Saints with the new generation of choir boys aiming, just as he had done, for the West wall.

It gave him his first West End success and an introduction to the luxury living of success à la Noel.

It gave him a reading list. 'Noel made me use my silly little brain.' Bennett, Maugham and Brontë were the first three authors Coward recommended: Brontë, Emily, *Wuthering Heights*.

It gave him the beginnings of wider fame. He was interviewed in Manchester for example, where – riding so high, in love, well off beyond his dreams, twenty-three, light years away from the bit part cadging days only three years previously – he declared that 'only fools are happy . . . I somehow can't get that way. I always examine things so closely that immediate pleasures are dwarfed by my insistence on ultimate benefits. . . .'

Only acting, it seemed, could reliably oust that ever-threatening despair. And Noel Coward's final and arguably his best gift to Olivier was, as he might have put it, 'in the acting field'.

Olivier's giggling was an unbecoming, unprofessional but apparently incurable nuisance. It was, as Olivier now says, a form of hysteria. The force of energy and desire which had shocked him into action as his father, totally unexpectedly, fired the starting pistol, and the sense of emptiness within himself he still felt, combined with an overspill of sheer activity perhaps helped detonate the hysteria. Coward would not have it. He said that he would cure Olivier of it and he did. Night after night he would try to make Olivier giggle on stage and whenever Olivier did so, Coward would 'kill' him – publicly humiliate him and later in front of the entire stage staff, dress him down. It was a very long battle: the young actor full of impulse and scared-stiff spirit but powerful, and the totally detached, professional, even classical Coward, able to wither anyone across the breadth of a stage. Perhaps only someone of Coward's determination and authority could have done it – for Olivier declares that it took about seven months. But he was cured.

He was twenty-three. His new wife was to come into *Private Lives* as it set off for New York where it would be a sure hit. He had rocketed to stardom and in the process apparently changed himself utterly. He was now the complete, debonair, matinée idol about town. To the life. He had changed himself and found himself. Professional to the last pluck of an eyebrow. And if Noel Coward ever dared try to make him giggle on stage he knew – as that boat set sail for New York – that he was now strong enough to outgun Coward and, as the term goes, 'kill' his teacher.

Below and overleaf: Private Lives with Noel Coward, Gertrude Lawrence and Adrianne Allen, 1930; and with Noel Coward on liner, returning from America.

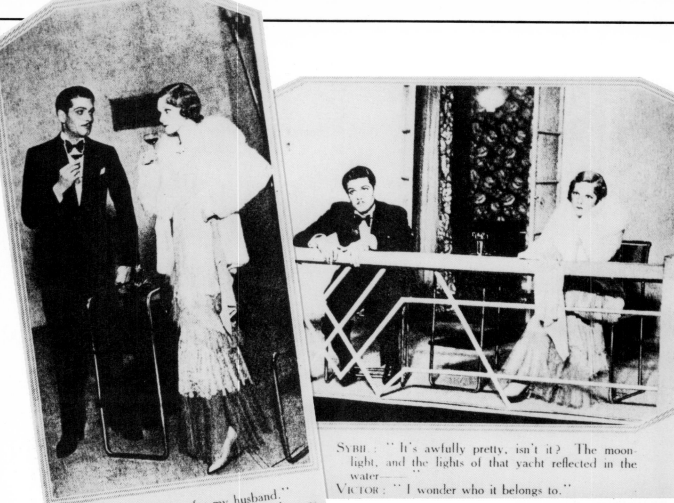

SYBIL : " It's awfully pretty, isn't it ? The moon-
light, and the lights of that yacht reflected in the
water——"
VICTOR : " I wonder who it belongs to."

SYBIL : " I was looking for my husband."
VICTOR : " Really, that's funny. I was
looking for my wife."
VICTOR : " To absent friends."
SYBIL : " To absent friends."

FAME AND HOLLYWOOD

There is a thirty-second strip of newsreel from 1931 which 'stars' Laurence Olivier and his new wife Jill Esmond. They are posed as for an official portrait. Their attitude is that of a couple representing some Very Important Institution. Appropriately for the times, it is the handsome young man who speaks, modestly, while the beautiful young woman maintains an equally modest, supportive silence. The location was Hollywood, RKO Studios.

'Ladies and Gentlemen,' the young, double-breasted Olivier said. 'May a comparatively young English actor offer his very humble congratulations to those who have initiated this enterprise. Hollywood has set a very high standard of production but I know perfectly well that the British brains and the British capital embodied in these and other British studios will make the British Picture Hollywood's most successful rival.'

Even at that stripling age, Olivier's sense of being English – the word 'British', you feel, was a committee's cautious corrective – had been noted, was being merchandized with himself as a willing agent. This undisguised and instantly, perpetually, available patriotism is clearly felt most sincerely: it is also a part he can assume, abroad or in a crisis; a part which, once again, takes the onus off himself, the empty bore he persistently describes his 'real' self to be.

When Olivier arrived in Hollywood – predictably yanked over from the success of *Private Lives* on Broadway – he came to a film industry rejoicing in the invention of the Talkies, mad for English accents and abounding in famous exiles from Chaplin to Ronald Colman.

Olivier had made himself like Colman. He had seen him as the man who could give him the eminence he lusted for. He had made a remarkable job of turning a gauche, skinny, rough, indiosyncratic quirk of a youth – as might be a young Heathcliffe – into the debonair, athletic, dewy-eyed charmer of the matinée crowd. Coward had sharpened him up. Jill had brought him firmly into Society; she was one of the best-connected, most talented, most desirable and loveliest of the young actresses. Coward was the wittiest and one of the most successful playwrights in the Western world but Colman was a universal star, and with Jill, Olivier said his farewells to Coward and set off to be greeted as a very possible second Ronald Colman. He saw the way the wind was blowing and let it take him. Colman was the key to the fame of the times.

Olivier has often said that he was 'greedy for life', that he wanted to 'eat it all up'. John Gielgud speaks with something approaching alarm of Olivier's wholehearted, forceful, even reckless seizing of a part and 'wringing its neck'. 'Terribly brave,' says Richardson, who chose his words with considerable discrimination. 'Didn't give a damn.' Only assumed characters can get Olivier out of the dungeon of his own Beckettian bleakness. And in 1931, Ronald Colman was all a young man could want to be.

The transformation and the original. *Private Lives*, 1930; picture postcard portrait, 1931; Hollywood studio portrait, 1932; Ronald Colman, Olivier's model, early thirties

Previous page: Fire Over England, 1937

So Ronald Colman he became.

He was also in love. From accounts of the time he was, like Romeo, in love with the idea of being in love. He seems to have fallen for ladies tall, small, older and younger throughout his Birmingham and early London days. He tippled into affections like a game pup getting into trouble. He could not help it, so it seems. A kind look, a charming smile, a pretty figure and whoosh, away he went, empty as a drum, longing to be taken over and played upon.

It would be surprising if his intimate life with Jill Esmond, as later with Vivien Leigh and Joan Plowright, did not have a significant influence on his public career as an actor. It would be surprising if there were not parallels, connections and crossovers especially as all three were at the very least accomplished actresses – in the case of Vivien Leigh a world-famous film star, in Joan Plowright's case a superlative theatrical actress – all of them intelligent, all of them strong-minded enough to have careers of their own and yet delighted to act alongside their husband whom all regarded, whatever the particular colour of their respective fortunes, as the superior talent. And insights galore could be had from knowing about those private lives, no doubt. In the most quiet, two-alone times is he the chameleon king or the nonentity – anonymous? Is control in public, that unknowable but undoubtedly colossal will to succeed, to dominate, to star, to attack, to be at the centre, is that balanced by or sustained and relieved by a tormented, unjust, insecure, unreliable, petty private face? There has to be some clay somewhere; and the rumours and the gossip, the malicious memories and the posthumous revelations, all conspire to throw a murk of innuendo over what may be rather simple and comparatively blameless. For he might indeed be a rather ordinary conservative chap who in a long and unusually testing life entertained three marriages – not all that remarkable in this day and age, even among apparently rather ordinary conservative chaps.

I have no way of knowing and such speculation is not within the bounds of this essay. There are certain assumptions it is reasonable to make – insofar as they touch on his career. His love for Vivien Leigh, to take one example, encouraged him to mount a *Romeo and Juliet* with her in New York in 1940 which was a terrible flop, took all their hefty savings and turned them to actions they might not otherwise have taken. His love for Joan Plowright, to take another example, appears to have stiffened his resolve to take the new ideas, writers and mood of the late fifties with him into his pre-National Theatre run up. Anything much else would be little more than idle chat. And, who knows? Perhaps the truth of it all is that he led his patently 'driven' life in some profound way regardless of the woman he was in love with, just as he led it despite, as often as following, the best advice and against, as often as for, his own apparent best interests.

It cannot have been the greatest fun for him to realize – swiftly

Above: Selling Olivier to the United States, 1931

Below: Olivier and Jill Esmond at Waterloo en route to America to meet Garbo

– that in Hollywood, Jill Esmond was widely regarded as the better bet of the handsome new English pair. Even the Ronald Colman lookalike job lasted only so long: soon his rather desperate American publicists were dressing him up in American sporting gear and attempting a repackage. In two years he made three films – none distinguished, none at all extending him – and he felt so underused that 'I even wrote a play. No good, of course.' Jill and he had been instantly adopted by the smart young Hollywood crowd which swung around with Douglas Fairbanks Jnr, a most sympathetic friend, who remembers Olivier as being 'known as Jill Esmond's husband. Naturally that didn't appeal to his sense of pride very much and it discouraged him a great deal. He wasn't getting many jobs.'

Lack of work stifled him. He could not bear it and to escape it did what some of his friends thought a very ruthless thing: 'Behaved like a shit' was one later comment. Jill was offered a star part in *Bill of Divorcement* by Selznick: Clemence Dane's highly successful, controversial play. John Barrymore was to be in it. It was the proverbial chance-of-a-lifetime.

Olivier wanted to go home and work in London. There was a film waiting for him with Gloria Swanson – *Perfect Understanding*. Jill went with him.

Bill of Divorcement was a smash hit, making its new leading lady – Kate Hepburn – into a twenty-two carat star. *Perfect Understanding* was a flop.

They resettled in London. A fashionable residence was acquired. Normal West End life resumed as quickly as possible.

Almost immediately Olivier received a request to return to Hollywood to co-star with – Greta Garbo. He accepted. Jill went with him.

The newspapers went mad: local boy made good; Garbo's charisma and mystery, her beauty and popularity. The chilled sexy way she said the words had made her 'world-famous'. It was as if our boy was being sent into the lists, or, more crudely, out to stud, so stridently did the British press proclaim their delight that Garbo had fingered Olivier and no other.

One of the characteristics of Olivier, during our interview, was the way in which he would switch his own roles as he told different parts of his own story. Nothing very unusual about that except, of course, that in his case both the switches and the echoed roles were more than ordinarily interesting. When he talked about his teacher, Elsie Fogerty, for instance, an affectionate tone, at once lightly mocking and lightly ponderous, summed up the picture of a woman of Agatha Christie or Margaret Rutherford bulk and benign intensity, shrewd though eccentric, acute but also helplessly open. When he spoke of being stifled during those two years in Hollywood when all he picked up were three undistinguished films, he literally strained back his head, unconsciously – it seemed to me – searching for breath: truly. As if he were remembering, re-enacting a literal withdrawal of the basic substance of life. I looked at it again on the unused rushes: exactly that.

When he talked about Garbo he first of all beat about the bush. He can be and he is retrospectively quite tough on himself. Some would say cleverly too tough thus forcing you to reconsider your own toughness and ameliorate it – but he was merely searching for the clearest, simplest expression of what was a woundingly clear and total rejection of him by the Great Swede. 'I wasn't up to it,' he said. 'I couldn't compete. I was out of my league and she knew it.' Even now, owning up is not so easy. Defeats dent confidence and confidence is essential, he has said, to acting: as essential before an audience as humility is before a text. Possibly he had not yet been able to uncover a sexual self able to deal with Garbo's demands.

Brutally given the Garbo heave-ho, he went to New York and repaired some of his hacked-down ego with what was widely regarded as a blindingly brilliant performance as a homosexual in *The Green Bay Tree*. Back in London he played Bothwell in *Queen of Scots* directed by John Gielgud and then took the town by the throat at the Lyric where he gave a Barrymore-Fairbanks-Olivier display of matinée swashbuckling and audience-grabbing pyrotechnics as Tony Cavendish in *Theatre Royal* directed by Noel Coward. That made him feel better: restored the balance a bit. Time to look around. Time to take stock. Sniff things out.

Left: With Jill Esmond in *The Green Bay Tree*, 1933

Above: Olivier as producer for the first time

Those who know Olivier well and have followed his career closely will always talk about his very sure 'instinct'. They, too, can be seen sniffing the air as they say it, associating it with animal wisdom as we all tend to do. Instinct, though, can be the intuition of an enormously wide range of information so tightly compressed and so forceful that its complexity and its urgency elide into a compulsion to act without waiting for what would be the enfeebling hesitation of analysis. We can only guess at the final powers of those who rise to the very great heights scaled by Olivier in a profession which is so volatile and finally dependent on that dark oracle called, variously, public taste, or mood, or whim, or fantasy, or even need: something like a current of air seems to bear them up. And it is part of their genius to discover it, part of their skill to ride on it, part of the age's recognition of them to seek them out in order to bear them up. It is a deep and binding pact you make with your times and maybe you have to sell your soul to get it.

Olivier had been Ronald Colman, but it had not taken him far enough. True he could command a high fee and a starring role in New York and in London; true he was still being sounded out with film studio big-dollar contract offers; true his contracts and experience were wide enough for him to consider launching into one of his openly declared ambitions – to be an actor-manager. All this at the age of twenty-eight might have seemed a good hand for most folk. But it was Olivier's undeclared ambition which now took over: the ambition to soar up into himself through the invented characters of others which he could employ for his own release and relief.

Since his marriage, the face, the character, the role, had not been greatly stretched. Though it was always addressing itself to new parts, new plays, new movies, with – judging from the reviews of the day – massive energy, with ingenuity, with exceptions, Olivier had taken on a pattern of roles woven around the matinée idol: he was the super-juvenile lead.

South of the Thames, at that time in a grubby old barn of a theatre near Waterloo Station, Lilian Baylis and, more importantly for Olivier, John Gielgud were setting out to prove to a widely sceptical and thought to be hugely uninterested audience, that William Shakespeare could be box office. By March 1935, Gielgud's *Hamlet* had recorded 155 performances, a number exceeded only by the legendary Irving. Gielgud in Shakespeare was the toast of the town.

Olivier saw what he wanted and went for it.

It meant risking a rattling good boulevard reputation: it meant a large cut in salary – particularly painful for Olivier who has never concealed his extreme carefulness with money any more than he has concealed his apparent enthusiasm to throw it around entertaining his friends or put it at extreme risk producing and backing his own West End shows which often as not crashed. He wanted Shakespeare though: he wanted the fame and he wanted the parts. In a sense, at this juncture in his professional life – the Garbo chop had been a very public, very humiliating rabbit punch: the movie world had not taken to his impersonation of a star – he wanted to go back to his professional roots, to his first success in the choir school, in those plays applauded by his mother and the fashionable theatre people of the day. Shakespeare – for him as an actor, lost, rather, in the flight to stardom – was home.

Gielgud called him in and it was with Gielgud – to the public's delight – that he was to fence. The elegant, intellectual, thoughtful and witty John Gielgud had a purity of dedication to the work he loved that had gathered about him a flock of acolytes. There was and is something priestly in him, something Roman, Jesuitical perhaps but not conspiratorial. He was overloaded with work and wanted someone to share Romeo and Mercutio with him. Olivier was his third or fourth choice.

As Romeo, it seems, they could scarcely have been more different. Gielgud – air and spirit; Olivier – earth and passion. The critics wanted air and spirit. Olivier was not so gently panned. He was told he could not speak Shakespeare's verse. 'Me?' He literally spluttered, remembering it forty-six years later. 'Me? Not speak Shakespeare's verse? I had been brought up with it. Me? I had spoken it all my life. Me? It was ridiculous!' And there he was, in his seventies, still struggling unsuccessfully to bottle up his indignation. 'What they meant,' he said savagely, 'is that I didn't *sing* it.'

Gielgud, who cheerfully and modestly admits now that he may well, indeed he may have 'sung' the verse, added, 'He was much more natural than I in his speech, too natural I thought at the time, but now I think he was right and I was wrong and that it was time to say the lines the modern way. He was always so bold: and even if you disagreed, as I sometimes did, about his conception, you had to admire its execution, the energy and force with which he carried it through.'

Peggy Ashcroft, who was Juliet to both Romeos, has described Olivier then as 'the definitive Romeo. A passionate sixteen-year-old boy in love with love.' Ralph Richardson, the wise owl of that generation, simply pointed to a photograph of Olivier underneath Juliet's balcony – 'the animal exactness, you see. Very fine.'

Olivier slewed his life around and faced up to Shakespeare.

Here began a series of transformations as radical as those which had turned him from a gawky student into a so-smooth juvenile lead. His Romeo is indeed, as Sir Alec Guinness recalls, 'remarkably beautiful'. Guinness, incidentally, who trod the same boards as Gielgud and Olivier, was then firmly in the former's camp, dismayed, as many were, by the matinée vulgarities – as he saw them – the tricks and tones from the commercial theatre.

But Olivier was not to be subdued. His reason for doing Shakespeare was not to win the appreciation of the Few –

although he appreciated that like any sane man – nor to seek the applause of the Many – though, again, he would try everything within the character to surprise and command the audience to respond. What he wanted was to act these great characters in such a way that he could believe in them. He did not want to go through any motions. He wanted himself to be moved in them, then others might be moved or not as they would. It was his own compulsion for a variety and depth of self-expression which turned him to Shakespeare. There he could and did find enough of himself to last a lifetime. Thus the extremely poised and coolly discriminating Dame Peggy Ashcroft, in considered recollection in her lovely Hampstead gardens about half a century after the event, still flashed with the memory that 'he *was* Romeo'.

Never one to miss the chance of doubling his bets, he starred in the film version of *As You Like It* as Orlando. In a tentative, unimaginative, stiff but by no means negligible movie, his light, sweetly serious interpretation stands up well. He disliked it: it finally convinced him that Shakespeare could never be done on film and helped lower still further in his eyes the status of a film industry which had failed to embrace him strongly enough. *Fire Over England*, set in the time of Elizabeth I but in prose and in full pursuit of a contemporary audience, was much more the thing that films could do. Vivien Leigh was his co-star. Her rise to national stardom had been dazzlingly swift: one night unknown, with a single small stage appearance to her credit, the next, the West End's hottest new name. She had had a crush on Olivier for some time; they fell in love in *Fire Over England*. At about the same time, Jill and Laurence Olivier had their first child, Tarquin.

In 1937, girded for the battle and wise to what he wanted, Olivier came back across the river into the Old Vic, and, to start with, Hamlet. After that he came on as Sir Toby Belch looking so radically different that the only way you could tell that it was the man who had played Hamlet, said one critic, was by his teeth. Hamlet had been arrived at through careful study with the director Tyrone Guthrie, poring over psychoanalytical interpretations, burrowing as deeply into himself as he dared. He was still criticized for his speaking of the verse and there were some barbs but overall the critics were 'fine', says Olivier. 'It was thought to be OK. I got the worst over first.' The public turned it into a huge hit. The beginning of what was to become a matinée-idol following for Olivier's Shakespeare interpretations was seeded here.

If Hamlet gave him the chance to exorcize some demons from his own fear-filled childhood, Sir Toby Belch let him loose once more as the joking, coarse, irresistible, grand master Twerp of the age. The contrast could not have been more dynamic, which is just what Olivier intended it should be. He was running a campaign and he was taking as few chances as possible: which meant, in his terms, to take as many risks as he could get away with.

Above: With first son, Tarquin

The campaign was to compel Them – whoever and wherever They might be – to know that he could and would and should play Shakespearean roles because he needed to and had to and was going to put himself in a position where it was his unassailable right to play any damned Shakespearean part he ever had a mind to whenever he chose to do so. Henry V was next, again directed by Guthrie, whose guiding intelligence greatly nourished Olivier as he yoked himself to these labours. For work it was. He did not like *Henry V* in 1937: he thought that the public might not like *Henry V* with all the thought of war and the rumour of war. At first Olivier appears to have attempted an anti-heroic Henry V and we can see in the photographs of that time little of the deeply confident, even swaggering, kingly qualities he brought to the role later. But once again it was a hit. 'Do you know why you are so good in this part?' asked Charles Laughton. No: why? 'Because you are England.'

Jill Esmond had been with him in *Twelfth Night*. When, at the end of the season, the company was invited to give *Hamlet* at Elsinore, it was Vivien Leigh who, out of nowhere it seemed, quite suddenly joined them and was Ophelia to his Prince. At Elsinore, too, it was a palpable hit.

He was not finished yet. He decided to do *Macbeth* with Michel Saint-Denis: again, as people tend to be when their talent and their boldness are united flat out and with a single aim, he was lucky in this director too. Saint-Denis told him to 'find the sense through the verse'. To this day, Olivier repeats it as if it were an incantation. Slowly, his eyes on the middle distance, moving his shoulders as if delivering a final conclusive line, 'You must find the sense *through* the verse. (Pause.) If that doesn't make any sense, sorry: it's the best I can do.' Iago was next for the operating theatre of Olivier's seemingly relentless display of strength and versatility and finally a Coriolanus which at last all the critics rose to. Directed by Lewis Casson, who had known and helped Olivier since he was a boy, the part brought out all Olivier's commanding manliness, his breathtaking stage acrobatics, his furious attack. He had conquered the London critics; he had bowled over the audiences; he had taken and was now living with Vivien Leigh; he had reached out for air and grasped greedily at Shakespeare to give him new lives. He was the chief lion of the pride, the new prince of the boards. See how he stands as Coriolanus: arms crossed, face granite, the undisputed victor, the Champion.

Then he left the stage to go back to Hollywood.

He had, of course – because there was and is a cautious side to Olivier, too, a belt-and-braces Olivier and also a workaholic and I'll-do-it-if-the-money's-right Olivier – made three films while he was laying seige to the characters in Shakespeare. One of them again co-starred Vivien Leigh – with whom he was entering into a lifestyle demanding far more cash than the Old Vic could ever offer – and on the two others he worked with his old friend and

Opposite: With Vivien Leigh in *Romeo and Juliet*, New York, 1940

Opposite: As Henry V

As Richard III

Below: As Shylock in *The Merchant of Venice*, 1970

Opposite top: As the Mahdi in *Khartoum*, 1966

Opposite bottom: In *The Betsy*, 1978

Opposite: Portrait of Olivier (it hangs in the Garrick Club)

advisor, Ralph Richardson. It was Richardson's advice he sought when offered the part of Heathcliff in *Wuthering Heights*. 'Bit of fame,' said Richardson. 'Take it.'

Although this is the merest speculation, it seems to me possible that the quite furious outburst of creative versatility at the Old Vic might have been ignited by his love for Vivien Leigh and her loving positive belief in him. He wanted to show her what he was made of, what a man she had on her hands. He wanted to show off. As she had – he has openly said – loved him more richly, far more richly, than anyone hitherto, and he her, so he wanted to open himself up, show her the power and the profundities, show her the glowering faults and the strength. Being who he was, he did this in the character of others and in public. No wonder those who saw those performances in the thirties at the Old Vic still talk vividly of how Olivier 'moved', 'struck', 'thrilled' them. He had opened up new cylinders.

But the call of the siren was not to be resisted.

Even though the part was Heathcliff, the producer Sam Goldwyn, the director William Wyler, the money good, the cast including his pal David Niven, Olivier hesitated. He wanted Vivien to play opposite him as Cathy. Wyler said no. He would offer her the second female lead – which, for an English actress unknown in America, would be a tremendous start, impossible to imagine a better. No, said Vivien Leigh, she wanted the lead or no part at all. And she had already announced to some friends that she was going to play Scarlett O'Hara – the most coveted female role in the costliest film in Hollywood's short, blockbuster history.

Olivier left her for Hollywood full of conquests: Shakespeare, Vivien Leigh, London, the British cinema. After a few weeks on the set of *Wuthering Heights* he was all but crying to go home. He had been humiliated, insulted, mocked and cut off at the knees by a director who thought he was artificial, operatic, snobbish and unserious about the great new medium of cinema. Olivier confesses to having behaved very badly: he was hoity-toity and unforgivably patronizing to Merle Oberon whom he saw fit to remind that she was not a 'real' actress; he called film 'this anaemic little medium which could not stand great acting'. He seems to have behaved like a spoilt and ignorant brat aping outmoded oh-so-English aristocratic mannerisms to emphasize a superiority that existed only inside his 'conceited' (his word) mind. Wyler flayed him alive, in public, daily, giving him nothing but the whip. After Take 32, when Olivier would be almost whimpering with frustration for some guidance, some note, some help, something, Wyler would pause, meditate and pronounce: 'I just want it better.' Or Wyler would mock, 'Which dimension do you think you're in now, Larry?' and constantly tell him he just didn't 'believe' in him. This, to Olivier, whose sense of his own identity depended on making himself believable, was intolerable. He became ill. He was petulant. But he listened.

And he took notice.

And today he confesses that Wyler was right and that he was an insufferable snob. 'You see, we – my lot – didn't take it seriously. We loved the The-a-tre. To us, movies were just for the money. Cinema to them was the sacred art.' And from that Olivier now concedes he blindly and blithely hammed until Wyler taunted it out of him. And now he is more than generous – grovellingly grateful – to his old tormentor who 'taught me how to act in movies: taught me respect for them: taught me how to be real'. The old Olivier inner calculator had not only been ticking along to clock up all those unpalatable new truths about film acting, it had also made a couple of surprising leaps. (1) That if stage acting looked phony and affected and unreal on the screen it might well be because most stage acting *was* phony and affected and unreal. This went into the Olivier bank and from then on he says that he drew on his 'P/W' (post-Wyler) film experience to help his stage 'reality'. (2) That anything at all could be put on film if only you could find a way. Wyler, at the end of the shooting of *Wuthering Heights*, invited the hurt, humbled and still squirming young Englishman to his house to dinner to bang him over the head one final time with that parting message: yes, even Shakespeare could be put on film if you could find the way. Remember that.

Wuthering Heights was a triumph. (Doubling up as usual, Olivier had a concurrent triumph on stage in New York.) He was now, at last – in a role which, ironically, drew most from that rough gypsy boy, pre-Jill, pre-Colman, pre-Coward – a massive and important Hollywood star 'with the right kind of spotlight

Above: With Katharine Cornell in *No Time for Comedy*, 1939

Left: With Merle Oberon in *The Divorce of Lady X*, 1938

Opposite top: With Joan Fontaine and Alfred Hitchcock filming *Rebecca*, 1940

Opposite bottom: With Edna May Oliver and Gia Kent in *Pride and Prejudice*, 1940

shining on me,' Olivier explains today, careful that you should appreciate it exactly, 'the right kind of success in the right kind of part.' When his beloved Vivien came, alone and afraid, to seek her screen fortune, he left Hollywood. In a repeat of his behaviour to Jill Esmond, he almost put a spoke in the wheel of Vivien's great fortune in landing the part of Scarlett O'Hara against enormous odds. Her long-term contract offer did not suit his purposes and he objected. He was told not to be 'a shit for a second time'.

Opposite: Coriolanus, 1938

Vivien, under the most colossal pressure and without Olivier, became an even bigger film star than he was. Ticker tape, world fame, celluloid glory.

He from his pinnacle, she from hers, they looked out for each other and tried to work together. She tested for *Rebecca*. A screen test exists and decently good as she is you can see why the producers would not buy her: she was much too sexy, lively, kittenish, mischievous for the part eventually taken by Joan Fontaine. Nor was she allowed to be in *Pride and Prejudice* – yet another distinguished hit for Olivier who now, it seemed, could do no wrong.

But they would play together. As lovers. In Shakespeare. And put all their money on it. *Romeo and Juliet* was a disaster and all their money went down the drain in Broadway.

War had already been declared. Too old to be called up in the first batch, Olivier nevertheless says, convincingly, that he hated his accidental exile, felt like a coward, felt 'ashamed, dirty, horrible'. He took flying lessons – although flying scared him – and got his licence so that he could go straight into the Fleet Air Arm – as he hoped – on his return.

His genuine and complicated guilt did not prevent him and Vivien – a newly married couple – from making *Lady Hamilton* before their return. This was to be, and proved to be, a propaganda film especially well thought of by Churchill – his favourite film, in fact – and by Stalin. (Hitler, on the other hand, was especially fond of *Fire Over England*.) Much of the reason for doing the film was to give them some money so that they could properly look after their various children and other dependents. Nelson's words were aimed as much at the Germans as at the French and his sentiments were unblushingly close to those of Olivier himself.

For his Englishness – his 'birthright' as he still calls it – never far below the surface, had swept him up, elbowing out all other acts and parts. He wanted to be back 'home', to be the Englishman he needed to be at this hour. Olivier and Vivien landed near Bristol and were driven to a bomb-shattered hotel so cold that they slept with their clothes on. It proved to have been a good idea. The sirens went in the middle of the night and they hurried for cover.

Olivier declared then and maintains now that after eighteen months of 'agony', he at last felt happy. He was 'home'.

Above: With Gloria Swanson in *Perfect Understanding*, 1933

Left: With Ann Harding in *Westward Passage*, 1932

Opposite top: With A. Bromley Davenport in *Too Many Crooks*, 1930

Opposite bottom: With Gloria Swanson and Nigel Playfair in *Perfect Understanding*

Laurence Olivier and Peggy Ashcroft

Opposite top: With Edith Evans and John Gielgud in *Romeo and Juliet*, 1935

Opposite bottom left: With Peggy Ashcroft – Olivier as Romeo

Opposite bottom right: As Mercutio in the same production

Above: As Sir Toby Belch in *Twelfth Night*, 1937

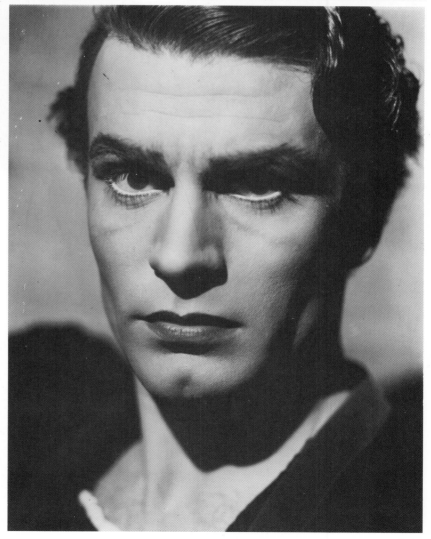

Right: In *Hamlet* on stage, 1937

Opposite: With Vivien Leigh in *Fire Over England*, 1937
Right: With Flora Robson and Vivien Leigh
Below: With Robert Rendall

I am torn with *Desire*...tortured by hate!

SAMUEL GOLDWYN
presents

WUTHERING HEIGHTS

co-starring

MERLE OBERON · LAURENCE OLIVIER · DAVID NIVEN · *Released thru* UNITED ARTISTS

with FLORA ROBSON · DONALD CRISP · GERALDINE FITZGERALD   *Directed by* WILLIAM WYLER

Below: William Wyler rehearsing Olivier and Merle Oberon in *Wuthering Heights* (film released 1939)

Opposite: As Heathcliff, with Merle Oberon

Above: Taking direction from
Alexander Korda in *Lady Hamilton*
(USA title: *That Hamilton Woman.*
Film released 1941)

Opposite: With Vivien Leigh in
Romeo and Juliet on stage, New
York, 1940

The Fairbanks friendship. On the boat to England, 1932, with Jill Esmond, Douglas Fairbanks Jnr and Joan Crawford; the farewell party for David Niven (guests include Cary Grant, George Sanders, Douglas Fairbanks Jnr, Ronald Colman and on his right, Olivier), California, 1939

Below: 3 September 1939, the day war broke out, with Douglas Fairbanks Jnr, California

SHAKESPEARE AND ENGLAND

'We will go forward. Heart, nerve and spirit steeled. We will attack. We will smite our foes – and in all our deeds in this land and in other lands, from this time on our watchwords will be "Urgency", "Speed", "Courage". Urgency in all our decisions. Speed in the execution of all our plans, and Courage in the face of all our enemies. And may God bless our cause.' The unmistakable voice of the young Fleet Air Arm officer bugled through the Albert Hall; the organ played 'Jerusalem'; the ranks of British servicemen and women swelled to match the moment. Cry Larry, England and St George!

If – as I have decided to – you opt for believing everything genuine that you feel Olivier has said about himself, then he was at this time desperately attempting to be anonymous. He was also determined to serve his country. He is convinced that he succeeded in the first and indeed if one looks at the casual, almost bland-faced, stocky photograph of the quiet-seeming man in uniform you can see what he was hoping for. He was disappointed that his strenuously won flying licence enabled him to do no more than ferry air gunners around safe skies in southern England so that they could learn how to keep in touch with base. He was an erratic pilot, it seems, and more than one, more than two aircraft hit the dust too hard for their frames. But he studied to be anonymous. 'The best part I ever played,' he says.

Which, of course, leads one to an assumption contrary to mine – that you must not believe anything he says because he is always acting. I believe Joan Plowright has said that he is 'always acting'. Her authority is scarcely to be questioned. But the conclusion must be that it makes little difference to the truth of his remarks whether he is 'acting' or not. Indeed, my understanding is that he can only express the truth of himself through the acting, just as he insisted that in Shakespeare you can only arrive at the truth through the verse. He is what he seems and he always believes it: that welcomed stamp of passionate, early faith is indelible. A favourite anecdote of this time in the Fleet Air Arm was once, when eating in the Mess, a senior officer was told that the young man down the table was the actor who had played Nelson. 'Nonsense!' said the senior officer, squinting carefully at the anonymous Olivier. 'Fella doesn't look a bit like Nelson.'

It was necessary for Olivier to be anonymous in order to do his job. He felt that the only way to survive was to assume the local colouring. 'I wanted them to think that I had been called by God into the Fleet Air Arm: that there was no other station in life I could possibly in any way fulfil.'

The new part was not only necessary for his survival and to ease what he saw as his new passage – as a serviceman. It was also an essential defence. It is easy to forget how very exposed, how very much at risk actors are: and in the truth emerging through parts and tales, incidents and anecdotes about Olivier, it is useful to remember that there is also a strong conviction of the necessity for reserve, for 'no show', for very English, very public school,

Opposite top left: In *The Demi Paradise*, 1943 (USA title: *Adventure for Two*); *opposite top right:* As Air Chief Marshal Sir Hugh Dowding in the film *The Battle of Britain*, 1969

Opposite: Fleet Air Arm officer Lieutenant Laurence Olivier with air scouts, August 1942

Previous page: The film *Henry V*, 1945

very stiff, emotional reticence. Olivier likes the character of the deeply shy conservative: it is always on the stand there, out in the hall, and you never know when he might not take it down and put it on. But he was well aware that in his films and in his stage performances, with those cries, those leaps, those sobs, those declarations and extremes of feeling – he had laid himself bare. Those people in the Mess knew him and he feared how very well they might know him. He went into anonymity like a turtle into its shell.

For this section of his life – the War, the roaring forties, the quasi-royal procession into the mid-fifties – I interviewed him back at the Old Vic. He was very pleased to be there. It was not one of his best days but he was well enough and he darted around backstage and on stage pointing out a feature here, cursing himself for extending the apron and 'ruining a perfectly gorgeous Victorian acoustic'. It was here that I had some intimation of just how much it takes, just how much you need. For he looked out into the empty auditorium sad and apprehensive. 'I'll never act on stage again,' he said. 'I haven't the guts. I haven't the nerve.' The risk and the insecurity of it all was all in that weary, sorrowful look.

We rarely see powerful people doing their work, which is most often that which both gives them and shows off their power. Great politicians, international businessmen, administrative mandarins, heads of departments, universities, corporations, states – all of them work largely in private if not in secret and we have intimations of their character only in gossip-column flashes or in rare moments of in-vision. One of the reasons we like our sportsmen so much is that we can see displayed before us qualities we all have but raised in them to a superlative degree and enjoyed by us because of the revelation of power play as much as for the sport itself. Even more so with actors, who test and risk their reputations and livelihoods before our eyes. Although the preparation, the thought, the rehearsal are all done before we are allowed in, nevertheless when we are allowed in we see the works. Not only the drama itself but the play of the actor in the character. And if we have been compelled to suspend disbelief, commanded by someone of Olivier's authority to believe in the truth of what he is doing, then we feel we know the man. We may be right. The man himself may – in Olivier's case fully admits it – give himself'. What he has given, though, if he has any range – and Olivier sought range, demanded versatility, refuses to have anything to do with the safe, predictable packaging which was so profitably wrapped around most stars – is many selves. In that range he revealed a lot that was not very comfortable. Not very nice. Not at all pleasant. More than a bit much. Best to roll into a ball of blankness in the Mess like a little hedgehog and push out all your quills: *noli me tangere*.

Yet there was a greater force and that was England. His patriotism – mistrusted by many of his friends – was freely on

Opposite and above: Taking Olivier back to the stage of the Old Vic, 1982; and his last time on that stage

tap, unlike tears which, he says, he has never been able to call up. England, at this critical juncture, called on everything he had to offer. I am sure he believed in every word, every ringing intonation of the speech that opened this chapter. England, over the next decade or so, England, and his place in it, was to be the unifying factor in his life.

Olivier wanted everything, as he has said. He wanted stardom in Hollywood: got it. He wanted the praise of his contemporaries in the great roles of Shakespeare: got it. He wanted one of the world's most beautiful and prominent women: got her. He wanted money: got it. He wanted to be a dashing West End idol: got it. He wanted to maintain his personal obscurity: just about got it. He wanted close friendships: got them. He wanted to be somehow aloof at the centre of it all: seems to have got that too. Now he wanted to be England.

In the War, he was asked to introduce this, to read the commentary on that, to appear here, to act a support there, to lend a hand, a name, a voice, a presence. He took it all on, and this feeling of himself as one serving his country, and through it realizing yet more hitherto unused reservoirs of character and energy, swept him into a period of quite stunning achievement.

In the twelve years between 1944 and 1956, he ran through great parts on the stage like a high-wire artist superbly teasing gravity: Richard III, Sergius, Astrov, Hotspur, Oedipus, Mr Puff, Sir Peter Teazle, Caesar, Antony, Macbeth, Malvolio, Titus Andronicus. He played with smaller parts, ornamenting them to unforgettability: the Button Moulder, Mr Justice Shallow, the Grand Duke of Carpathia. In the cinema his three Shakespearean films made history, as they say, and the cliché was apt: *Henry V*, *Hamlet*, *Richard III*. Nor was that enough: he starred in William Wyler's *Carrie*, he starred in Peter Brook's *The Beggar's Opera*, he starred opposite Marilyn Monroe in *The Prince and the Show-girl*. And moreover. With Vivien Leigh (who was Cleopatra to his Caesar and again to his Antony, Blanche in his production of Tennessee Williams's *A Streetcar Named Desire*, Sabina in his production of Wilder's *The Skin of our Teeth*, Antigone to his Chorus) he went into management and ran the St James's Theatre, having been ousted from the Old Vic, a company which he, Richardson and Burrell built up to world standards as a repertory company fit and ready to be the launching pad for the dreamt-of National Theatre. We are not finished yet. There were projects he started and despite even his energy failed on – the film of *Macbeth*; there was a midnight birthday dinner party given him by Churchill; there was a knighthood and a tour of Australia where he and Vivien Leigh took a 'royal' salute. Fans lay out all night in the streets in the rain to see him: he was mobbed after performances of classical power and integrity; he was the greatest actor, they said, married to the loveliest star in the whole damned world, and then he took on Marilyn Monroe. And that was not the end of it. He got himself Notley Abbey – against advice from Vivien and most of his friends – and set himself up in this twelfth-century Augustine monastery with seventy-five acres and a full, belted, high-style English landowning nay aristocratic county life complete with house parties, digging out clogged-up ditches and a model farm. He lived the lives of many men then and it was England which both released him and kept him together, which unloosed his greatest versatility, which at times seems to have made him incredibly arrogant, overweening, power-seeking, autocratic, dictatorial, ruthless and at other times ushered in a pastoral and patient tenderness. Shakespeare was the pivot.

Above: With Vivien Leigh in *Antony and Cleopatra*, 1951

'As far as I was concerned it may as well have been the first Shakespearean film. So far as I was concerned it *was* the first Shakespearean film.' *Henry V*. So far as the public is concerned he is right: it is the first Shakespearean film.

In his constant battle to stave off boredom – which is a kind of death – Olivier employed many tactics: one was the surprise attack. He went out to surprise his audiences with the histrionic leaps, the sudden falls, the great cries. He constantly and often alarmingly surprised his fellow actors. 'It's like being on stage with a cage full of lions,' said Anthony Quinn. Most of all he yearned to surprise himself. And so after William Wyler and Carol Reed had been approached and been unable to direct the film, Olivier decided, in 1944, to direct this expensive, difficult and important film himself. He had never directed a film before. He would also produce it. Oh, and he would take the leading part. And, moreover, do the adaptation, take work of William Shakespeare and take it on himself and cut it down to size. It would all be very surprising indeed.

Olivier, though, at that time, doing something for his country which, however obliquely, he knew was in some way what his country needed, was on song. Again and again in *Henry V* Olivier's ideas, Olivier's control and Olivier's ambition thudded into the bull's-eye. He was worried, for example, about the 'unreal', 'unnaturalistic' Shakespearean verse in a medium seemingly – at that time – bound eye and tongue to naturalism, to realism. His answer was brilliant. He would give the film an opening – in, as it were, Shakespeare's old Globe Theatre – of such High, even Camp theatricality and artificiality that when the cameras swung away into real landscape, the relief of getting out of that theatre would cushion the equal artificiality of verse spoken in natural surroundings by men acting in a realistic convention and mode. Throughout the film, whenever possible, the scenic effects are highly theatrical, even fantastical, not unlike the illustrations in *Les Très Riches Heures de Duc de Berry* which Olivier consulted: and, he hoped, that heightened background would deflect attention from the foreground making it easier on the ear of conventional forties cinema-going expectation.

But that was just the beginning. He made the fights look like fights, the battle look like a battle, he opted for a way of shooting a long monologue which went directly against the prevailing wisdom – i.e. the camera pulled further and further out as the verbal intensity grew whereas the Commandment until then had said the camera should go further and further in. He shot the open-field sequences in Ireland and some of his most self-enjoyed anecdotes are about that time and his tussle with the Irish farmers who brought their own horses for £3 10s. a day, who wore the chainmail knitted by blind nuns and challenged 'Mr Oliver' as they called him to show them the way to do all the acrobatic bits, which he did and badly sprained an ankle, dislocated both elbows, bruised this, jolted that. He charged around the Irish

Above: With Vivien Leigh in *Caesar and Cleopatra*, 1951

Above: Preparing to film the cavalry charge in *Henry V*

acres either waving a sword at the head of an army or pointing a megaphone, in charge of a film crew. Like all highly successful men in what are basically cooperative ventures, he took great care to surround himself with expertise and loyalty. Reginald Beck advised him on technical matters; Dallas Bower, who had already done a script of *Henry V*, was brought in as associate producer; Robert Krasker was the cameraman; William Walton did the music; good and reliable actors filled the major roles; and the whole enterprise was nursed by an extraordinary little Italian co-producer, Filippo del Giudice, who adored Olivier, was unshakable in his belief that a masterpiece was being created, shielded his man totally from the slings and arrows of outrageous backers and was the eventual recipient of Olivier's special Oscar. 'Without you, dear fellow,' Olivier said, '*Henry V* would never have been made.' There was never any lack of style.

Henry V was a success in England and a triumph in America. It made money. It gave Olivier a unique place in the cinema's pantheon of great actors. It introduced many, many people to the work of Shakespeare. It was excellent propaganda. And still today it stirs the blood while Olivier – who rarely allowed

himself more than a single take even for the longest of speeches –
comes across with unfailing heroic conviction. 'We happy few . . .'
indeed: those who made it.

If *Citizen Kane* is rightly reckoned the most astonishing first
film ever made, *Henry V* has a serious claim to run it second.

But Olivier was basically an actor and before *Henry V* was
released he took on another high-risk venture. He was to co-
direct at the Old Vic alongside Ralph Richardson and John
Burrell. And he would take on the big roles. He had glamour
enough from *Wuthering Heights*, *Rebecca*, *Pride and Prejudice* and
Lady Hamilton. Now he wanted the glory.

To loosen up a bit, he and Richardson took *Arms and the Man*
out of London. Olivier was playing Sergius. When Tyrone Guthrie
complimented him on his playing, Olivier retorted angrily. How
could he be expected to play such a stupid, unlikeable fool as
Sergius. 'You have to love him,' Guthrie said, 'or you'll never be
able to play him.' Olivier has several times mentioned that this
struck him deeply: certainly he went on to play Sergius to huge
acclaim. At last, Olivier has said, he understood something both
profound and practical. Yet it seems to me he had always known
it. It's curious. For the same thing had happened to him in the
thirties with Henry V until Richardson had gently led him to love
that blatantly heroic king. And again and again Olivier had difficulty in actually liking, much less loving, the people he was
expected to play. His dislike, even hatred, of them was often
expressed in the fulminating, rather blustering language of the
public-school dormitory – what beastly awful rotters they were,
what dreadful chaps, really! It was as if he could not admit
anyone into his inner being unless he loved them and yet he
could not give what he wanted to the act of playing them until he
loved them. Once admitted, he could feed them. But it was a
jealously guarded cave, that empty centre still full of terror and
loss, still desperate, compulsive for another life to appease it or
anaesthetize it. Anyway, Sergius was a hit.

He had begun his second career at the Old Vic with the
shrewdly modest little part of the Button Moulder in *Peer Gynt*.
This was a great triumph for Richardson, who was also in his
greatness as an actor and fully able to stand firm against the
torrents of his old friend. It was very nicely calculated. There he
was, the great film star, the great patriot, the great idol of the
London stage of the thirties – and oh, look, he had taken on such
a very little part so as not to stand in the light of the great beams
coming from Richardson. Then Sergius – totally different – a
transformation so complete that, were it to happen in Hollywood
today to one of the current film actors, there would be an
international conference called upon to admire it. Olivier did it,
business per usual, without fuss. His audiences knew him now:
his differences were their pleasures.

Then came Richard III, Shakespeare's crookback, since mourned
and criticized by fervid companies of scholars who declare that a

great poet did great injury to a great King: but the play survives and Olivier was one of a long line of English actors who, through the centuries, came to *Richard III* as full of expectation and apprehension as he himself came to Bosworth Field.

Olivier's use of make-up has often been remarked on. In his quest to be different he must have slapped pounds, even tons, of putty and greasepaint onto his features. The nose is what he tends to go for. His principle is that it is better to change one thing radically than attempt an overall reshaping: and the nose is the easiest game. He has never stopped changing his looks and, incidentally, changing his shape; heavy exercise at last released his reborn limbs to the air and in some photographs he looks quite musclebound – once again a feat of will for a man whose metabolism and inheritance leans decidedly towards slightness. The nose in *Richard III*, though, became, through the portrait by Salvador Dali, through the photographs, through the film and the *réclame* of the part, almost a character in its own right with an existence of its own, a Gogolian, monstrous nose. But it was only the start.

There was the limp. A limp given unwarranted help during the filming – ten years later – when an arrow fitted with a warhead and intended for the flank of a steel-plated and protected horse instead went through Olivier's calf. Then there was the humped back. And the voice – a thin, donnish reed was selected from the

Above: Salvador Dali with Olivier as Richard III; and two noses: King Lear, 1946; and Sergius in *Arms and the Man*, 1944

quiver of possibilities, partly because it was far away from the sound of Donald Wolfit, whose Richard III, well received, still surged about Olivier's senses, partly because the donnish reed seemed so far away from the full-blooded evil of the man.

The 'look' of Richard III illustrated yet another aspect of Olivier, and one which he speaks of defensively. That is, his admission that he builds up a character through externals. He is always accused and humbly accepts that he is the epitome of the anti-Method. One clear source of inspiration, it seems, for Richard III was the American theatre producer, Jed Harris, 'the horridest, vilest, cruellest man I ever met'. Jed Harris had directed him in the *The Green Bay Tree*. Harris seemed to provoke virulent dislike in many quarters: even the Big Bad Wolf was modelled on him.

All those easy explanations and relaxed analyses were in the future, however, when Olivier faced that first night as Richard III: the renewal of his life-giving struggle with Shakespeare, a basic embrace/conflict which he has been engaged in now for almost seventy years. He knew – because his antennae catch all the messages on the wind – that the audience and the critics out there were waiting for him. And, in his dressing room, he feared that he was cracking up. He did a most curious thing. He called in a friend, John Mills, whom he knew was in the audience and told him that he could not remember the lines, that he could not get the character, that he was going to give one of the worst performances of his life and would he, John Mills, please go around and explain and apologize to his friends for this terrible mistake and disaster that was going to happen in about ten minutes.

If my notion has any truth in it, then what was happening was Olivier's realization that he would have to show the nastiness that was in him. And to do that he would have to live the crook-backed, evil man. If it is true that he allowed himself no real character of his own but sought to piece it together through the creations of others – just as he himself pieced his characters together through the observation of others – then he was having the greatest difficulty swallowing Richard. He knew that on the other side of fear lay relief – for at last that particular part of him would be given life – but he was also creating monsters out of himself and perhaps there would be not only relief but a permanent addition to his character. If Henry V left him in some way forever heroic, might not Richard leave him malevolent? He has spoken about this, lightly but keenly.

'You probably have some venom in you . . . you may be a venomous character to a certain extent, probably I am . . . I may have all sorts of vices, in fact I'm sure I have, but through the medium of acting you can get rid of an awful lot of that . . . and I think it's absolutely permissible in acting terms . . . it's like a confessional almost, you're confessing your sins, which is a great relief to the soul . . . you're using your performance . . . I think that's alright.'

Richard's malevolent, power-seeking, cutting, crippled, cruel vision of life was there, in him, to be called on and he was almost hysterically afraid to summon it up. But by the time he had limped onto the stage, ten minutes after the confession to John Mills, that profound metamorphosis had yet again taken place, and Olivier gave a performance which dazzled and stunned the London audience.

He was to live with that Richard III on tour and then in the film for about the next ten years. It could be argued that its effect on his own character was more disturbing than anything else that happened to him during that time.

He decided to film *Hamlet*. Once again he would do everything – the script, the directing, the acting and all the stunts, including the longest sword fight in screen history (over 300 mostly vicious passes). Olivier never gave an inch in fights: you went for him or he went for you. 'The only way to make it look real,' he said. 'And you have to have a gift for it. You have to enjoy it.'

He set himself an entirely different set of objectives in *Hamlet*, filling it with the artifice of the camera, glooming it in atmosphere, in the process having to exclude one of the key monologues. An old friend who worked on it with him observed at the time how definitely Olivier snapped in and out of roles: at a certain time of day he was the producer; then he was the director; then he was the actor; then he was the script consultant; then he was the editor. On the set he seems to have had no time for discussion: he knew how he wanted every movement, every inflection, every rhythm and the job of the crew and the company was to do as told. *Hamlet* brought him even more *réclame* than *Henry V*.

The English critics – once their textual qualification had established their literary credentials – purred: the American critics swooned. Even Sam Goldwyn rhapsodized. Crocodiles of children were once more trailed through the streets to see Shakespeare in their favourite context. Hollywood laid out four Oscars. Olivier got his knighthood. Richardson already had his. We are told that Olivier was furious that Richardson beat him to the honour. We are told that Richardson rang him up, when offered his, to assuage any natural jealousy and that Olivier congratulated him warmly. Whatever and what matter about all that, the knighthood gave Olivier very great pleasure: he still prefers Sir Laurence to Lord Olivier. As a knight of the realm and the Prince of Denmark, he and Vivien Leigh had become theatre royals. From Mayfair to Melbourne, from country house to country lass, the glittering brilliant talents, seen to be a smiling charming couple who had begun in an enviably risqué manner as lovers but redeemed all by marriage, international success and stout war effort, were now idolized . . . they were an ornament to the nation.

Meanwhile, down at the Old Vic, Olivier continued to plunder himself for a series of varied parts. As Astrov in *Uncle Vanya* he 'found' the character in a pince-nez. As Hotspur in a ginger wig

Below: Knighted, 1947

he had a death scene so dramatic that there were those inclined to
discount the whole of *Henry IV*, Part I in anticipation of that
spectacular fall. He was by all accounts a most athletic and
terrific Harry Hotspur, a lad fit for war and fun. As Mr Justice
Shallow he was all but unrecognizable, an old maid of a man, so
full of business that he threatened even the unrolling majesty of
Ralph Richardson's mighty Falstaff.

Richardson spoke of his Shallow with great affection. 'Laurence
said – why don't I keep bees? I said – good idea – Shallow lives in
the country – let him keep bees. Well, that was all very fine but I
would be saying something and – slap! – a bee would sting him
and – slap! – there would be another one and – well! – buzzing
about everywhere. Now look here, I said, we can't have you
going on like that. I have a lot of plot to get through here. If you
carry on like this I shall just – bumble off. And he smiled his
sweet smile and said, OK Ralphie, I'll bee-have. And he did.' And
then he was a thundering King Lear.

On one double bill his versatile virtuosity glowed out like a
pair of Chinese dragon eyes, facing out of a cave, daring challengers
to come in and challenge. He played Oedipus in Sophocles'
Oedipus Rex and, having left the stage with bleeding eyes and a
howl based on his imagined reproduction of the pain a fox felt
with its leg caught in a steel trap, he reappeared fifteen minutes
later as the ridiculously liveried, powdered and pomaded, flighty
and sparklingly superficial Mr Puff, to be hoisted and shot and
cannonballed around the stage like a rag doll. 'It was vulgar,' he
says now, 'showing off.' As box-office it was, yet again, bull's-
eye.

For Olivier was now doing something quite extraordinary. To

the classics and to a company of serious actors, he was drawing the numbers and enthusiasms of a matinée crowd. When he took the Old Vic Company on a tour of Australia and New Zealand in 1948, the sendoff in London and the reception down under were both fan-filled; show-biz – front page!

In Australia he led a company through a most exhausting and difficult tour. He remembered every birthday. He attended every laid-on cocktail party. He made pro-British speeches. He took the salute at a march-past. He played his great parts to astonished audiences and his wife batted alongside him blow for blow. Just as the Old Vic, with its unexpected, Lilian Baylis, uniquely theatrical Englishness provided the right setting for his burgeoning as the greatest actor on the English-speaking stage – Gielgud, with enormous and characteristic generosity had handed over to him Edmund Kean's sword for his Richard III – so this tour of Australia was to be the training ground for the future National Theatre Company. For that was what Olivier had his sights on and that is what he was moulding. Indeed that is what it was, in all but name, as the tour swept through the cheering colony and the crowds slept out in the streets.

Then he was fired. Right then, in the middle of the tour, between performances, on the other side of the world, he got a letter saying that he, Richardson and Burrell were fired. Olivier even today can't quite believe it. He still laughs with astonishment. 'I mean – we'd built it up. We'd made it what it was, the three of us. You know – I think they were jealous.' It appears they thought that Olivier and the others had got above themselves, were too much the stars, were using the Company for their own ends. That action probably set back the opening of the National Theatre by ten years – more – and what a National it would have been if Olivier and Richardson had led their young troops – most of whom, since then, have made great reputations – into that battle.

Still, he was fired. Not that it took effect right away: no, he had to come back and do another stint at the Old Vic, during which he transformed a deficit into a thumping profit.

By now Vivien Leigh had clearly found herself the resources to take on major roles and the strength to stand up to her husband on stage. She had scored a remarkable success as Sabina in Thornton Wilder's play; she was Lady Teazle to his, unusually subdued, Sir Peter, and then she was Antigone. Olivier directed and played the Chorus in what became a very unexpected success. They were flying in their professional lives, although rumours were afoot that their private life was under great strain. Vivien Leigh's health was certainly under strain and when Olivier agreed to direct her in *A Streetcar Named Desire* there were those, like her friend John Gielgud, who feared for her in such a role.

'You see, it was so very like her, in a way. It must have been a most dreadful strain to do it night after night. She would be shaking and white and quite distraught at the end of it. Perhaps it

Above: Olivier, Vivien Leigh and Old Vic Company leaving for Australia, 1948

Opposite top: Olivier as Astrov in rehearsals for *Uncle Vanya*, 1945

was unwise to let her do it.' She had tuberculosis and suffered from mental strain. She drove herself remorselessly.

But it seemed the two of them were employed in a perilous game of urging each other on to greater and greater tasks, higher and higher risks, their mutual and independent ambitions now intertwined, now opposed, driven on, both of them, from different roots, by different demons, to burn up the moment. They were locked in some extraordinary sorcery of play, competition and lust for incandescent experience in drama and perhaps in life. Jilted by the Old Vic, they determined to remain the royal pair of the London theatre and went into management at the St James's with a dash and extravagance that made a mockery – was it intended to? – of Olivier's widely confessed and often noted meanness. He was still trying to build a great company, still had visions of leading it into a National Theatre, lost money regularly and recouped only when he and Vivien came into the bullring together. They were Caesar and Cleopatra, they were Antony and Cleopatra, and although the critics in London were far from totally enthusiastic – and Kenneth Tynan said some penetratingly wounding things about Vivien Leigh, even accusing Olivier of chivalrously bringing down the standard of his acting so as to make hers seem better – in New York they enjoyed unalloyed praise.

With all this, Olivier was still ample enough to pursue his rediscovered Englishness in less intense ways. He had a small part in *The Magic Box*, for example, as a baffled London bobby, in which he showed himself the personification of all the good old London Gilbert and Sullivan bobbydom in the world. He scandalized the serious-minded by taking on, leading in and directing *The Sleeping Prince*, but he loved Terence Rattigan and he could see a boulevard smash hit when he saw one, old hand at that, and it was. He spotted new talent in Peter Brook whom he encouraged to direct *The Beggar's Opera*, disappointed only that Brook's singlemindedness did not let him contribute enough. But he played and sang and rode to the hilt (so violently that he gave his horse a heart attack) and did not sulk when what had seemed a lovely spry project turned into a dark commercial disaster. In Australia he spotted Peter Finch and took him up and took him on board and in the maze of private intimations and man-oeuvrings may well have known fully what he was doing.

Above all, though, there was, throughout this period, Notley Abbey. It was here that the many lives of Laurence Olivier came home to roost. Douglas Fairbanks Jnr was a regular house guest. 'I suspect he envisaged himself riding in and out of it in full armour . . . the place had such romance, almost theatrical romance, like a set.' And Gielgud found his friend played many parts. 'One day he was the landowner, one day he was the squire, one day he was the gardener, one day he was the great host. I was always rather fascinated. He does enjoy playing a number of roles off the stage as well as on, I think.' And what fun it must have been for

Above: With Herbert Wilcox while filming *The Beggar's Opera*, 1953

82

him. Though the compulsion might often be strangulating in its demands, there must be days when the faculty of being multitudinous must be something to revel in: such a sweet revenge on the mean trick of this one life we are given and given in such a way that the more we learn how to live it the less time and energy we have to do so. At Notley he planted his colours – the Englishman for all seasons.

There was at the end of the forties, early fifties, more than a murmur of criticism which accused Olivier of being too technical. James Agate articulated a prevalent anxiety when he wrote, 'When I look at a watch it is to see the time and not to admire the mechanism. I want an actor to tell me Lear's time of day and Olivier doesn't. He bids me watch the wheels go round.'

When we were filming the profile of Olivier, almost all the actors we spoke to referred to his technique. All praised it. All, at the same time, seemed to suggest that it covered a certain emotional void. In as polite a way as I could, I put this to Olivier, who did not take it at all well. We left in the film much of what became rather a wrangle – with him winning hands down of course and eggs streaming down my face by the dozen. But we left it in for two reasons. Firstly because it provoked into life a side of Olivier which we had seen nowhere else – a tetchy, defensive, even angry, even crushing side. For whatever it's worth, we thought it worth showing. Most people would – and did – blame me for the mood anyway and besides there are miles of him being, as he is, charming, funny, as Agate also said 'a comedian by instinct . . .' (the sentence completes itself '. . . and a tragedian by art'). Secondly, though he had denied any especial cleaving to technique, he went on to confess that his resentment at the line of questioning came because he had so often been criticized for his technique being a substitute for feeling. And he was most vehement that he did feel, he felt all he did, he felt it as strongly as he could and, looking around, as strongly as anybody else. But his job was to portray the character for an audience and in order to build up the character he collected and used effects, that was the only way he knew how, that was his method but it was all in the service of the truth of the character.

Looking at the scene again I find it rather distressing and almost wish we had cut it out. Because, I think, we were quite near the bone; also because he was by no means on top form that day, off balance a bit through fatigue; and partly because he wanted to protect the method which had been so flaringly successful in his professional life. To suggest that there was 'nothing inside' was to hit very hard and to seem to score. For the one actor who did not refer to Olivier's technique, perhaps the actor who knew, appraised and loved him best, Ralph Richardson, had a commanding grasp of Olivier's 'great greatness' as he called it, but would point to a photograph and after a paen of affection point further and say 'totally bored'; or end an excursion on a series of great parts by saying 'he didn't give a damn'. He knew the fear of emptiness at the centre. But he also knew – as I believe – that it is the fear of emptiness and not emptiness itself, and that when Olivier protests that he feels as much as anyone, he is right. Indeed he feels as much as everyone he plays, for all of them were summoned in to take him out of himself.

As if realizing that a great span of awesome achievement were coming to an end, with the instinct once again which marks him out, he swung his forces around in the mid-fifties. In 1955 he went back to the scene of his first triumph, back to the fount of his many characters, to the mould of his many masks, Stratford-on-Avon, where he played Malvolio, a titanic and shattering Macbeth and a Titus Andronicus which horrified audiences so much that nurses were called to stand by. As if marking some as yet undrawn line in his career, he did an extraordinary thing at the end of the last performance of Titus – a massive part which, alone, would have totally drained most actors. He stepped forward and thanked the company and all the technicians, by name and denomination, ninety-seven of them.

And then came Marilyn. The Knight and the Garter. *The Prince and the Showgirl* – a reworking of Rattigan's *The Sleeping Prince*. It was a publicist's and press paradise and a producer's hell. Olivier was the producer. Marilyn Monroe became the sex symbol extraordinaire, an angel of sex, an unexpectedly gifted comedienne; the American way of life, gushing up from squalid poverty through soft sex, celluloid and a sporting hero – Joe DiMaggio – to screen power and the netting of the intellectual playwright Arthur Miller. Marilyn Monroe was well known to be delicious, wonderful, box-office; rare; and a director's nightmare. Olivier was the director. Her rows with her studio, her sudden but real ambition to educate herself – into acting, thinking, culture, the works – rode badly on her body-perfect-public-sensational-sensuality. She insisted on her own dramatic coach, she would go for take after take after time-wasting, money-wasting, spirit-wasting take until she got what she wanted. She seemed to like to begin by wearing down her leading men. Olivier was her leading man. She operated entirely by a tight-shut inner motor which let her and her alone into its secrets. Olivier expected things to be done on request, on command, even the spirit could be conjured up by the will. Leave her alone, said his oldest friend and wisest mentor, Sybil Thorndike, who was also in the film; she knows what she is doing. But Olivier wanted to exercise his control. For many years now he had honed it and strengthened it and practised it on himself and others and it had worked again and again resoundingly. He brought into play all his considerable patience, all his immense courtesy, all his incontestable charm, but he still wanted her to do what he wanted her to do when he wanted her to do it. She insisted. She too was fighting with her life.

She won.

It marked the end of surely one of the grandest chapters in the career of any actor.

Above: Promotional still for the film
Henry V

Right: As Henry V in stage
production, 1937

Opposite: As Henry V in the film

Above: With Vivien Leigh in
The School for Scandal, 1948

Right: With Vivien Leigh in
The Skin of our Teeth, 1948

Opposite: Watching rushes of *The
49th Parallel* (USA title: *The
Invaders*) with Vivien Leigh, 1941;
and as the trapper in that film

Above and left: With Ralph Richardson and as the Button Moulder in *Peer Gynt*, 1944

Opposite: As Justice Shallow with Miles Malleson, and with Ralph Richardson (as Falstaff) in *Henry IV*, Part II, 1945

Above: Directing Jean Simmons as
Ophelia, in *Hamlet*
Opposite: The film *Hamlet*, 1947

Right: Olivier delivering 'To be or
not to be . . .'

Above: Olivier plunging on Claudius in *Hamlet*

Right: Olivier striking Ophelia (Jean Simmons) in *Hamlet*

Opposite: The duel sequence from *Hamlet* with Terence Morgan as Laertes

Following pages: Directing *Richard III*; playing Richard; and the death scene

Opposite top: With Peter Brook, the director of *The Beggar's Opera*, 1953; and, bottom, as Macheath

Right: With Sybil Thorndike in *The Prince and the Showgirl*, 1957

Below: With Vivien Leigh on stage in *The Sleeping Prince*, 1953

"THE SLEEPING PRINCE"
LOP 301

001 01

DIRECTOR   CAMERAMAN
LAURENCE OLIVIER   JACK CARDIFF

INT: NIGHT

DATE. 7/8/56

Marilyn Monroe filming *The Prince and the Showgirl* (adapted from the stage play *The Sleeping Prince*); with, below, Olivier directing

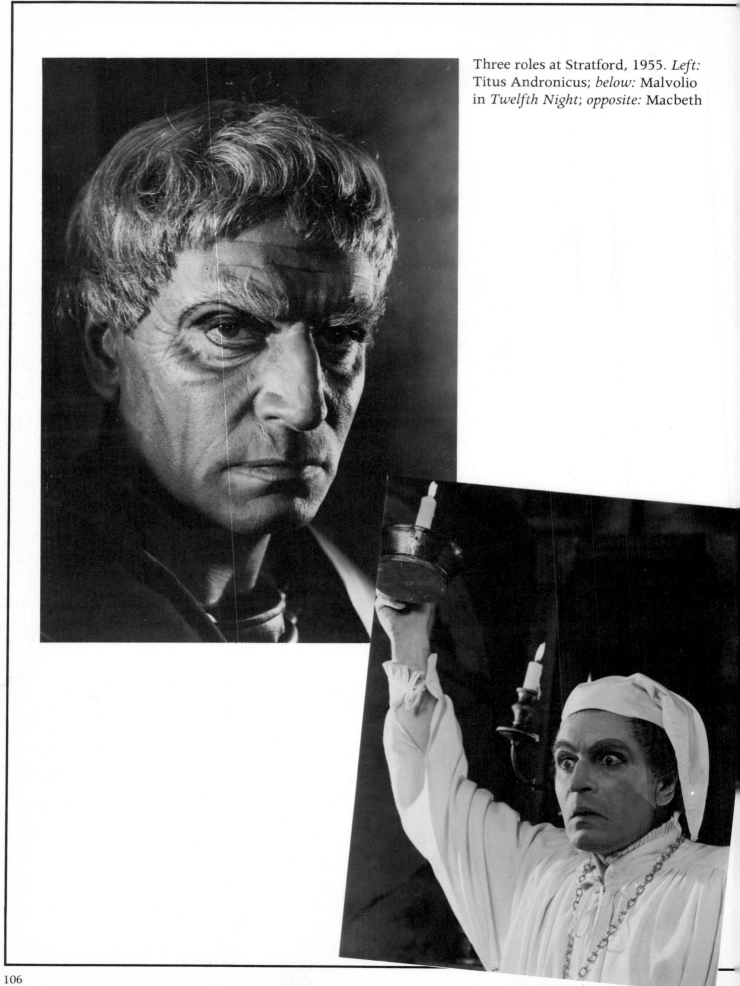

Three roles at Stratford, 1955. *Left:* Titus Andronicus; *below:* Malvolio in *Twelfth Night*; *opposite:* Macbeth

B2-61

'THE ENTERTAINER'
AND THE NATIONAL

By a fluke I have four key views of Olivier's next major move – which was to take the role of Archie Rice in *The Entertainer*. One from Arthur Miller; one from the author, John Osborne; one from Joan Plowright and one from Olivier himself.

While Marilyn was filming in England, she and Miller were virtually trapped by the press. This may have accounted, in some way, for her own 'unprofessional' behaviour on the set. It was all but impossible for them to move out of their rented country house without running a gauntlet of flashbulbs, leading a Keystone Cops steeplechase of press cars through the country lanes of England, and ending up with a night-out blighted.

Arthur Miller wanted to go to the theatre. To get Marilyn Monroe to a London theatre without causing a traffic jam and a riot in the foyer seemed impossible. And he wanted to see this new play *Look Back in Anger*. Firstly he liked the title. Secondly he looked down the list of plays on in London and all the rest seemed 'that awful English polite stuff' or revivals of classics. And finally, when Olivier told Miller that he, Olivier, had seen *Look Back in Anger* and loathed it 'because it was an affront to England', that clinched it: an affront to England was precisely what the weary, besieged husband of Marilyn Monroe most wanted to see.

Olivier fixed it. Cars roared out of different exits at the same time with lookalikes prominently installed. The press hared about after the decoys while, as in the very best thrillers, the real car with the real people sped out quietly when the coast was clear. The Royal Court had been most discretely pre-warned. Three seats were kept empty in the back row. The car circled Sloane Square with Marilyn bending her head as if scrambling for a contact lens and Olivier waiting for the start time to pass. Curtain up was held for a couple of minutes and while the punters coughed nervously in the dark, the three musketeers slipped in the back. Similarly at the end of Act One the house lights were held while the three of them scampered away to have a private drink with George Devine and so on until the end when they met Osborne himself.

Miller greatly admired the play. Olivier greatly admired Miller. During that little drink after the show, a most diffident Sir Laurence – pillar, column, monument of an Establishment on which Osborne's play poured vitriol for its hypocritical, empty, gutless, nerveless shams – gave the young playwright to understand that if ever he should come to have a part that he might think that he, old Larry here, might be able to tackle, then he would be very obliged to be given first refusal, very obliged indeed. Miller is very pleased to tell that story: it is part of his evidence that Olivier is the only actor he has ever known who 'matured'.

'It was a remarkable thing to do,' says Osborne. 'Quite remarkable at the time. People don't remember. There were those who warned him against the risk. And it was a risk. The part of Archie

Previous page: As Archie Rice in *The Entertainer*, 1960

110

Above: Osborne on Broadway, 1958

Rice seemed to go against everything he stood for – and certainly I did and certainly the Royal Court did. But he came along and did it. It was very brave. He was far and away the first of all that lot to notice that something was going on.'

'We thought that to act you had to wear jeans,' Joan Plowright said. 'Anybody very well groomed or too well dressed for their own good – we suspected all that.' The Royal Court was self-consciously, confidently and successfully radical. Olivier's arrival was regarded with some misgivings. 'But as soon as he rolled his sleeves up and started working with us it all fell away,' Joan Plowright went on. 'You can't argue with someone who can act you off the stage whenever he feels like it. You just can't argue with that sort of talent.'

'I was in a stew,' says Olivier, 'and I needed a change. It was big classic stage part, film, big classic stage part, film; I was boring the public, I was boring myself, I was predictable as hell, and it was a wonderful, wonderful part.'

There are those who think that he has never been better than he was as Archie Rice, the failure, the lecher, the empty clown, the song-and-dance man full of tired public gags and exhausted private pain. Olivier loved the part, he researched for it in the music halls, he found himself in it: 'I could have been Archie Rice; I could have joined a chorus and called myself Larry Olivier and been as happy as a lark at first.' He dazzled even its author at rehearsals with his cornucopia of inventiveness. In one bound he entered the New World of British drama and refreshed himself mightily.

But another failure further helped to define his position. He tried with all his considerable powers to acquire the comparatively modest sum required to finance a film of *Macbeth*. Despite the artistic and box-office successes of *Henry V*, *Hamlet* and *Richard III*, despite his success in other films and his proven popularity on the stage, it was no go for the Scottish play. Olivier's greatest declared pleasure – to produce, direct and act in a film – was now put behind him. That game was up. From then on he increasingly took cameo roles or small parts, like Crassus in *Spartacus* or the third lead, General Burgoyne, in *The Devil's Disciple* – in both cases, however, stealing the reviews from the expensive Hollywood muscle employing him.

And he was not going to let anything go. In 1959 Peter Hall directed him in a *Coriolanus* that had the critics racing for their most burnished superlatives and audiences again turning to the black market for tickets. He had one foot planted firmly in the new – in the same year as he played Coriolanus he filmed *The Entertainer* – but he kept a hold of his classical nurse just as he kept a way open to the American purse. He always did want everything.

The awesome thing is that, to an outsider, he very nearly seems to have got it. Most people whose talent or luck imposes its image strongly on the world have a brief shine of it, or fix themselves in a predictable firmament holding onto what got them there in the first place. Olivier's lustre seems never to diminish and never to stand still. When you look at a list of his credits, his roles in the theatre, his parts in film and on television, the plays he has directed, the films he has directed, the plays/films/television he has produced, the companies he has run, the business careers he has had, the public service career he has had, the private lives, the long friendships . . . there cannot have been his like.

He has said that Joan Plowright was the woman he found to replace his mother who died when he was twelve. He was almost fifty when he met Joan Plowright, already then an outstandingly accomplished young actress whose dedication to the theatre and steady sense of the radical movements of her own generation put her in a unique position: a complete pole apart from Vivien Leigh it might seem. They married a few years later when both their divorces were through.

If he had needed any encouragement to apply himself to the new course he saw opening up before him, then Joan Plowright was there to give it. There is a sense in which, by marrying her, he united the two most powerful factions in the British theatre: his own – the knight of the old glamour, the War, great roles, household names and honours galore; and that of John Osborne – young artists turning to the theatre to practise their art and display their genius but also to force society to listen to them, to make the stage into a pulpit as much as a playground. A new morality was loose and Joan Plowright was one of its most distinctive representatives.

The course he saw before him was based on two families. His own, with Joan Plowright and a house in Brighton, young children waving at the window as he went off to the station, a regular household just like the one he used to know as a child. Family snaps now capture Olivier as the new family man. And he wanted a theatre family. He had brought one into existence two or three times: now he was going to rear a family which would have a permanent existence as the National Theatre Company of Great Britain.

But he would not cease from the endless life-giving compulsion to surprise and to activate himself through taking on other characters. After Coriolanus, he swung through 180 degrees to play M Berenger in Ionesco's *The Rhinoceros*, directed by Orson Welles. Another hit. You look at him as the bloodlusting warrior, you then look at him in Ionesco and you wonder anew at the dynamic which was still sending up such forceful pulses for renewedness. And then to Anouilh's *Becket* and from that sub-dued almost inscrutable fanaticism to the whisky-stinking priest in Greene's *The Power and the Glory* for American television.

His first step in front of television – in 1958 as John Gabriel Borkman – had been attended by the sort of press coverage given to a world cup football final and the thunder throughout the land of television sets being turned off. Needed more concentration than anything else, he concluded, this newfangled television business. Needs fullest possible attention. So *The Moon and Sixpence* for NBC irradiated the American screen and sprayed him with raves and another new public. Nor was his mischief any less active. When Anthony Quinn left *Becket* after playing Henry II to Olivier's Saint, Olivier instantly grabbed the Henry II role and gave it such a seeing-to that the critics squealed with delight and, unfairly, pointed up Olivier's quicksilver versatility by contrasting it with the plodding interpretation of the departed Mr Quinn now gnashing his teeth in fury as he addressed himself to Barabbas. Olivier played Henry II in the biggest theatre in New York to packed houses while through the days he rehearsed and shot *The Power and the Glory*.

In 1961 he married Joan Plowright and was appointed Director of the Chichester Festival Theatre. That a very small county town most inconveniently situated for London should decide that it could sustain a theatre was rum enough: that it enticed the world's leading actor and a host of master players to come down and get it going was more than rum. It was to be a practice run for the National.

The trouble was it leaked. Or rather, it was announced that this Chichester team was going to be the basis for the long, long awaited National Theatre, and all the fun and sympathy that Olivier and his glittering troupe might have expected from this gallant country enterprise was swept aside as the microscopes bore down on the embryo that dared threaten to become the full-bodied National Theatre at last.

It's an odd world when something we are so provenly good at as a nation and something which gives pleasure to millions, employment to hundreds, exports well, brings in foreign capital and visitors, is precisely what we need to be doing in this post-industrial day and age, should have to batter its way through an ignorant and philistine government and bureaucracy as if it were an importunate outcast. Out to serve his country as he was, Olivier was to spend the next twelve years being a battering ram, a butt, an object of scorn sometimes and suspicion too often: but he did it. He hauled the National into existence and despite his final failure to lead his troops into the South Bank HQ itself, no one doubts that the National is perhaps his most enduring monument.

Not that it seemed much of a prospect in 1961, especially as the first two (of three) productions were slammed. Fletcher's *The Chances*, which he directed, and *The Broken Heart*, in which he played Bassanes, brought on the 'Is this what we are to expect from the future director of the National Theatre?' and drove out the Chichester audiences back, back into the pastures from which they came. Chekhov rescued him. Chekhov, Michael Redgrave, Joan Plowright, Joan Greenwood, Sybil Thorndike and Lewis Casson – his guardian angels – and himself as Astrov in *Uncle Vanya*. 'Perfection.' 'A wonder.' 'A masterpiece.' A cannonade of praise drowned the earlier cries of anxiety. After a bit of a wobble, he was on his way.

Meanwhile he clocked up two parts which showed his devotion to the new mood of the time: the wrongly accused schoolmaster in *Term of Trial* and Fred Midway in David Turner's *Semi-Detached*. Neither was well received. Neither was enjoyed by Olivier. Neither gave his sharpest critics much comfort about his judgement.

Above: Olivier appointed Director of the Chichester Festival Theatre, 1961

He asked the sharpest critic of all to come and join him. Kenneth Tynan, international apostle for hedonism, theatre critic extraordinary, taste maker and reputation breaker, had given Olivier some of his finest notices and some of his most wounding criticisms; he had mauled Vivien Leigh and hurt her feelings badly; he had championed John Osborne and was champing to find a battleground where he could clash prominently with prevailing attitudes which were, as he saw it, ridiculously puritanical, restrictive, ill-bred and hypocritical. It is typical of Olivier's sense of what was right for the purpose in hand that he was persuaded – he gives Joan Plowright the credit for this – to take on board the flag bearer of the New. It is a further tribute to Olivier, as much as to Tynan, that the younger man accepted. But then, as Peter O'Toole and scores of others have attested, when Olivier wants you to do something, he is hard to resist. Tynan was on board, which meant that the fledgling National Theatre would have range, it would have intellectual justification for what it did and it would have controversy. Olivier may well have given himself the shot in the arm he needed by employing Tynan: it could also be argued that it was Tynan's influence which crucially allowed him to lose his power base inside the company hierarchy and, in an apparently gentlemanlike fashion, be shown the door when he was owed, and in bucketfuls, much better treatment than that.

Above: Olivier with Kenneth Tynan, 1975

And so in 1963 the National Theatre centre of operations moved to its final staging post – a Nissen hut beside the Old Vic. Olivier brought in the hot young Peter O'Toole to secure the maximum bums on seats for *Hamlet*: he himself gave his Uncle Vanya and took a small part in *The Recruiting Officer*, thus demonstrating that he could be absent, dominant and supporting. Treble top. A very politic opening and a good season. *Vanya* was filmed as an increasing number of his stage performances were to be from now on. Though the quality of those films varies, they are never dull and at best seem to provide a good record of the production.

In 1964 he took on 'the impossible one': Othello. He had long thought it unplayable. Orson Welles had just got near it, he thought (in a production Olivier had presented in London), but 'he lacked the breath'. In a controversial career (controversial, that is, as well as everything else: it was also a classical career, a career of majestic unfolding, a conservative career in some instances, now and then an erratic career, in some ways a supremely purposeful career) this was to be one of his most disputed roles. Even his faithful Sybil would have none of it. To others it was the very summit of artifice. To those who played in it with him it could be devastating: one dazzled night they lined the narrow corridor behind stage and applauded him back to his dressing room. He slammed the door on them. But why, they asked, when you were great? 'I know,' Olivier said, 'but I don't know how I did it, so how can I repeat it?'

Zeffirelli said that the performance summed up 300 years of acting.

He took exercise. Weights. Jogging along the Brighton sea-front. Voice classes to get a whole new octave. Make-up taking three hours. Made discoveries of vanity in Othello, of intellectual pretension, of visceral jealousy. Loped like an African hunter, played up the African, an outsider still now in a white European society, and had to shield himself from plaudits and brickbats both.

In the same year he swung north to Halvard Solness in *The Master Builder*. It is quite tricky to think up a bigger contrast. It was to prove Olivier's most frightening role.

That dressing room he retired to was also his office. One of his leading actresses was also his wife in a full and happy spate of breeding and rearing a family. The workload he was giving himself beggars belief. Only someone who could lead several lives simultaneously could hope to survive it. Olivier seems to be a man whose energy feeds off energy, whose strength is given voltage by powerful achievement. The danger is that if you miss a beat, miss a footing, reflect on the peaks you are scaling so scarily, then the abyss and the attraction of the abyss can open up to suck you into it.

It happened for Olivier on the first night of *The Master Builder*. His throat clenched, the audience – including Noel Coward, Kenneth Tynan, John Dexter, Bill Gaskill, the press, friends, fans – went round and round ('anti-clockwise: why is it always anti-clockwise?'). He could not remember the lines. Even now, when he reinvokes it, something of the panic is clearly visible, clearly branded on his memory. He walked back, he got out one line, he thought of coming to the footlights and apologizing 'Ladies and gentlemen, I am very sorry but I am rather ill and . . .', but there were those out there who would never forgive him and never let him forget; nor would he, he was convinced, ever act again if this terrible blankness, this sudden nothingness were not to be filled with something.

His third child had been born. He had everything he wanted.

Maybe it was here, after the colossal strain of Othello which drained every gram of his forces (and remember, he maintained it was 'impossible to play', yet he played it); after the great happiness of the third safe child; after the cruel over-activity of running the young National but the great feeling of knowing it was on its way; maybe it was here that he relaxed and, for the first time since the terrors of abandoned adolescence, looked plainly into himself, the Master Builder. And found a most terrible, terrifying void.

He got through the performance, but for the next seven years it was liable to strike at any time. Strategies were employed to help him. He could not bear to be alone on stage and so in Othello's great monologues, for example – for the disease raced through all – his Iago had to stand in the wings where Olivier/Othello could see him or he simply could not do the part. When he felt the black about to strike he would summon the company and beg forgiveness for his unprofessional attitude but ask them not to, never to, please not to look him in the eye because if he caught a glance direct he would be finished. He fought it with the weapons of a man in an African village fighting against the fell judgement of a witch doctor. At the same time, he started on what was to be a long and grave run of physical illnesses.

But he went on. He took the Company to Moscow and, dressed as a steward, welcomed them all on board the aeroplane. He took the Company to Berlin and, as always, after an exhausting performance, stepped forward to thank the audience in the language of the land. He directed Arthur Miller's *Crucible* and O'Casey's *Juno and the Paycock*. As Tattle in *Love for Love* he pulled out a circus bag of slapstick and as Captain Edgar in Strindberg's *The Dance of Death* he delivered a performance of such force (recorded on film) that, for example, Gielgud considers it his finest non-Shakespearean role. He directed a *Three Sisters* memorable for its intense unity of style and for Joan Plowright's radical and realistic performance. He took a small part in *A Flea in Her Ear* because among the other thousand and one things he had to show – 'if you are an actor or a boss you have to get out and prove it' – was that he could be a good Company man. And every night of his life he was stalked by the terror of that black and bottomless pit which could open like a trap door and leave him silently howling and straining against the force of nothingness.

In 1967 he became involved in a bitter, wounding and draining fight with his own Board. Kenneth Tynan wanted to put on *Soldiers* by Hochhuth. It was an attack on Churchill which claimed, among other things, that the death of General Sikorski in an air crash in 1943 was an act of sabotage against the Free Polish leader, an act connived in by Churchill. No evidence was produced for this. Lord Chandos, Chairman of the National Theatre Board, a member of Churchill's War Cabinet and a friend of Churchill, would not have it. In his bones, in his background, in all his speaking for England, you feel that Olivier himself would not have it either. But he backed his man Tynan and he fought for his right to have complete artistic control. The correspondence, the passions and the injuries were all considerable. Olivier showed quite exceptional nerve and loyalty in working against an Establishment he adored and cherished. He lost and perhaps he was unwise to put so much into a battle which he surely knew he could not win. But he was someone who led from the front and went on until he won or dropped.

In the same year Vivien Leigh died.

It was also in this year that a cancer tumour was discovered. With quite foolhardy recklessness he insisted, at first, in having his heavy treatment as an out-patient while still holding up his Atlas-load at the National. But his health broke down.

Typically he turned his attention and his will onto the cancer to 'beat the bastard'. He succeeded. The tumour died away.

Above: Olivier as Director of the National Theatre

His greatest roles during this period were perhaps off stage: the administrator and the family man. The administrator can be seen in any number of photographs, with co-suited colleague administrators. The building of the South Bank theatre dragged on. His one five-year term was to turn into a second five-year term – all the time being forced to show how commercial he could be, how grand he could be, how National he could be, how bureaucratic he could be. Whenever they were attacked – which was often enough – Ken Tynan would always point to the record: in their joint time there they had more and, it could be argued, a higher quality of successes than any other theatre in the United Kingdom. Olivier planned and waited; paddled in the sea with his children; scooted off now and then to make good his extremely modest National salary with a film or two. He took part in *Bunny Lake is Missing*: so equally regrettably, did Noel Coward. He was the Mahdi in *Khartoum*: that was more like it. And Premier Kamanev in *The Shoes of the Fisherman*: that was not.

So bent to the great wheel of the National was he that his best performances on film were either in the recordings of the stage productions (*Dance of Death*, for instance, is electrifying) where he had already worked over and worked through the part; or in cameos (Field Marshal Sir John French in *Oh What a Lovely War*, Sir Hugh Dowding in *Battle of Britain*, Creakle in *David Copperfield*, Count Witte in *Nicholas and Alexandra* or the Duke of Wellington in *Lady Caroline Lamb*). In all these cameos he offered something definite: just to look at that particular gallery of cameo faces is to appreciate – even in a still photograph – the singularity

Below: With Richard Attenborough while filming *Oh What a Lovely War*, 1969; *right:* With Noel Coward in *Bunny Lake is Missing*, 1965

of each characterization, the effort made to get it right and get it different. It is possible that the cameos were so much better than the longer parts precisely because of his integrity. He could not bring all he wanted to the longer roles and so delivered muted, disappointingly unlively portraits. For the sprint of a few minutes' screen time he could group his forces effectively: and strike off a likeness.

His working day was from 10 a.m. until midnight. Its bookends were the London–Brighton trains. In his ten years at the Old Vic, there were seventy productions. He appeared in nine of them and directed eight – not much evidence of greed there. He was forcing himself to be a Company man. Yet it has to be said that the parts he took on were generally very big and tended to figure regularly in the rep. This made financial sense. He was the best box-office the National had and when a deficit threatened or happened, an Olivier lead would fill up the till. But much of his time was committees, architects, planners, local government, unions, craftsmen, estimates, budgets, designers, bills, hirings. In his hirings he seems to have followed the practice of young Prince Hal when he became Henry V: old pals from around the camp fires of the old days, the great old Shakespearean movies, the grand old times of the thirties and forties Old Vic, all the old faithful were not invited to the National party. He was starting afresh.

There were those – Tyrone Guthrie was the most prominent – who mourned this immersion in bureaucracy, seeing it as necessary for someone to do but possible for many to do, whereas Olivier acting in full maturity was something unique and to be cherished. There were others – John Osborne was the most articulate – who regretted Olivier's wasting his time on anything so museum-bound as a National Theatre and further regretted seeing him deliver himself into the ideas of Ken Tynan whom Osborne accused of 'intellectual spivvery'. There were good men who left the National and good men who did not try too hard to join. Yet, taken all in all, it is very doubtful whether anyone else could have done a better job. More to the point, it is highly unlikely that anyone else would have been given or been able to do the job at all. Olivier made his calculations, as he always did, as he did, his elder sister said, from a very early age, before he uttered any opinion. He saw his great role as that of the actor who conjured up the National Theatre. Nobody else had done that. Done once, nobody else could do it again.

On stage he played both A. B. Raham in *Home and Beauty* by Somerset Maugham and took the part of Chebutikin in *Three Sisters* which, with *The Beaux' Stratagem*, he took to Los Angeles in 1970.

In the same year he became the first actor to become a peer of the realm. Lord Olivier. He has never liked the ring of it, but he does like being a Lord: just as he loves having a railway engine named after him.

Above: Honoured by British Rail,
6 June 1980

And in that same year he played Shylock in a nineteenth-century setting of *The Merchant of Venice* and the following year let rip in a gigantic *Long Day's Journey into Night*. As in *The Entertainer*, Olivier found much in himself for James Tyrone: it was an elegy to someone else he might have been and a roar of pain at the thought of that damnation. As Antonio in *Saturday Sunday Monday* he romped through a production which saw Joan Plowright yet again command the applause of critics and audiences and finally, with all the irony available, he came to play his last stage role in *The Party*.

Trevor Griffiths' play about the schemes and principles, the paranoia and desperate politics of the far Left had as its hero John Tagg, a man who was civilizations away from Olivier, and yet he took on the long, taxing part at a time of great personal stress willing, to the end, to demonstrate that he was as committed to the new as the old, to the political as to the passionately private, that his National Theatre could contain multitudes.

He relinquished his post in 1973. He resigned. The theatre was not yet completed and he would not have the glory of taking his Company into their home. It was a cruel disappointment and, one thinks, more than a bit mean and small and lacking in generosity of all those concerned that they could not find a way to enable him to carry the torch those last few symbolically clinching steps.

But it is there. He more than anyone else put it there. A splendid auditorium bears his name. He rarely goes. His last work there was in 1974, when he directed his wife in a play by J. B. Priestley – *Eden End*. It could have been an epitaph.

Above: With Joan Plowright, Alan
Bates and Brenda de Banzie in the
film of *The Entertainer*, 1960

Right: Rehearsing Archie Rice

Opposite: In *Becket*, 1960

Above: Orson Welles directing Olivier in *Rhinoceros*, 1960

Left: With Joan Plowright in *Rhinoceros*

Opposite: With Maggie Smith in *Rhinoceros*

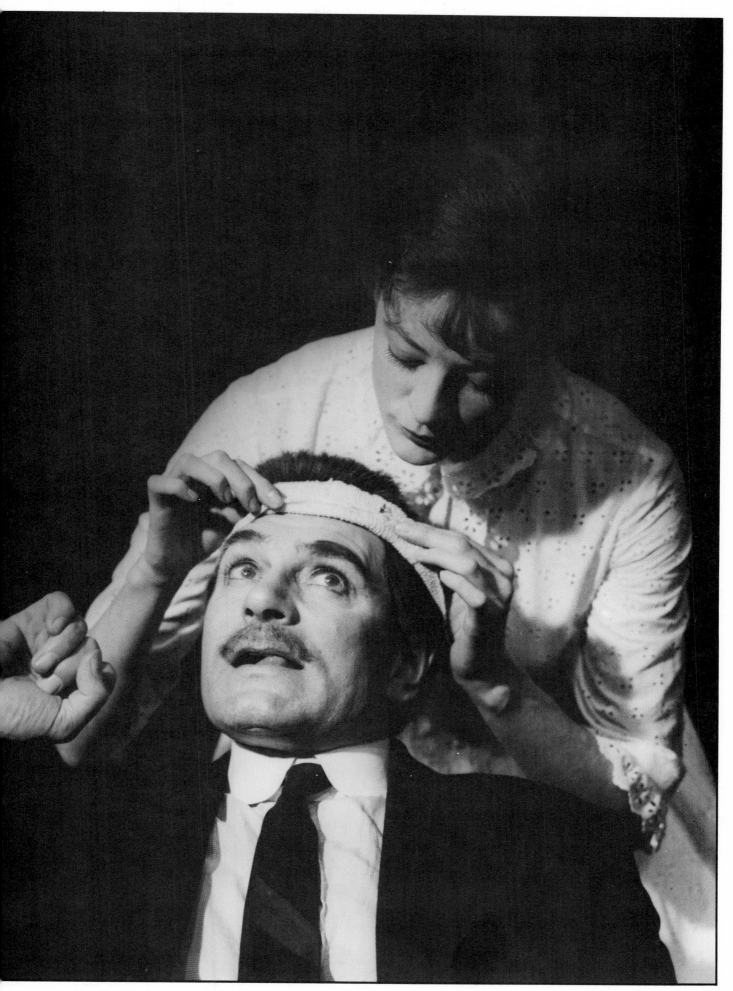

Two *Uncle Vanya*s. *Top left:* As
Astrov, 1962; *above:* With Margaret
Leighton, 1945

Left: With Sybil Thorndike in *Uncle
Vanya*, 1962

Opposite: As Othello, 1964

Below: With Miles Malleson in *Love for Love*, 1965

Opposite: As the Duke of Wellington in *Lady Caroline Lamb*, 1972

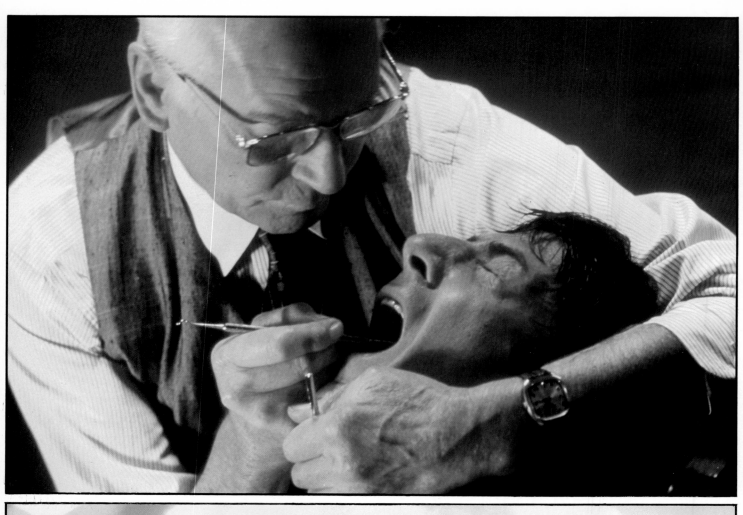

Opposite top: In *Marathon Man*, 1976, with Dustin Hoffman

Opposite bottom: In *Marathon Man*

Right: In *Sleuth*, 1972, with Michael Caine

Below: In *Sleuth*

Left: In *Brideshead Revisited*

Opposite: In *A Voyage Round My Father*, television, 1982

Below: In *Love Among the Ruins* with Katharine Hepburn, television, 1975

Opposite: In *Clash of the Titans*, 1981

Below: As Edgar in *The Dance of Death*, 1967

Top left: With Joan Plowright and Derek Jacobi on the set of *Three Sisters*, 1967

Above: With Joan Plowright in *Three Sisters*

Left: Directing Derek Jacobi in *A Woman Killed with Kindness*, 1971

Opposite top: With architect Denys Lasdun and a model of the National Theatre, 1967

Opposite bottom left: Olivier and Peter Hall, 1973

Opposite bottom right: After Olivier's last stage performance at the Old Vic, 1974

Opposite: With Constance Cummings in *Long Day's Journey into Night,* 1971

Right: A Flea in Her Ear, 1967

Below: With Frank Finlay and Joan Plowright in *Saturday Sunday Monday,* 1973

SOLDIERING ON

The next eleven years, which provide the shortest chapter, were probably, in many ways, the most anguished and slow, drawn-out time of Olivier's life. He became critically ill, recovered and then ill again and again. He had lost the nerve and the guts to act on stage ever again – very hard, for someone who had fed and fed off a live public since boyhood. He considered that he had failed his greatest test – taking a Company into the National. He had a young family to look out for and a world of hire and fire staring him in the face with no institute to shield him and no guarantee of health to support him.

He has often been criticized – several times over the years for taking unworthy parts in poor films, particularly in this period which saw, some would say alas, *The Betsy*, *The Boys from Brazil*, *Dracula*, *The Jazz Singer* and others. Olivier will always defend his acceptance of cameo roles and now he needed to service other characters more than ever before, perhaps. For his own essential physical character seemed to be breaking down: 'It was a kind of uproar in the cells,' Joan Plowright has said, 'and a sort of nervous breakdown, I suppose.' It threatened and broke, withdrew, regathered force and hurled itself on him again like the physical manifestation of that vertigo of stage fright which might well have been the advance messenger.

If – as seems possible – he lived many of those years in the shadow of death then there is a supplementary explanation for those roles: he wanted to leave his young family properly provided for. The money at the National had been sufficient for a quiet life but scarcely enough to leave an overflow for securing the future of young children. And despite Olivier's undoubted carefulness, even meanness, about petty savings, there are also many proofs of his generosity. When there is that sort of fear the need to ensure as cushioned as possible a future for your dependents must become urgent. He was looking after his own.

In amongst all that, because the man is and always will be a surprise and a star, he did some films which no one need be ashamed of: most of the world's actors would give their eye-teeth to have been half as good as he was in *Marathon Man*. While in *Sleuth*, as Andrew Wyke, he pulled off such a succession of tricks and tributes, such a 'Comstock Lode of experience' said Joseph L. Makiewicz, the director, that he had seen nothing to equal it in forty years. Most actors would have rested up for the remainder of the decade on the strength of it.

One of the many fascinating things about Olivier is that whenever he seems remotely to be typecast, or cornered, or in a rut, a pattern, a slide, he will see a way out and quite suddenly pounce on it. Now, unable to force himself back onto the stage and unhappy with the roles he could command on film, he swung his attention around to television. In America he enjoyed *Love Among the Ruins* with George Cukor and Katharine Hepburn. But it was in Britain, at Granada Television, that he found a home, a substantial base and one worthy of him. He was given a brief to make

Previous page: As Lord Marchmain in *Brideshead Revisited*, television, 1982

a selection from great twentieth-century plays, to produce them all and act in whatever he chose. This resulted in some quite marvellous work, especially his performance with Alan Bates in Pinter's *The Collection*. Once again, Olivier seized on a centrally contemporary playwright and funded the character with such richness that you catch yourself smiling throughout at his delight in himself, in the part, in the man he is showing you he is.

Nor was he afraid – was he ever? – to challenge comparison with others, as when he took on Big Daddy in *Cat on a Hot Tin Roof*: he had not the heft of Burl Ives, perhaps, but he was a Big Daddy all right.

And he was Nicodemus in Zeffirelli's *Jesus of Nazareth* and a wonderful bicyclist in *A Little Romance*. In many of these later roles he seems, usually sportively, to be trying on different versions of old age for size, rather as he might be trying on different suits. What sort of old man shall I be? Spry? Ugly? Mean? Sanctimonious? Ever so humble? A little vicious? Lovable? Unrepentant?

Below: With Alan Bates in *The Collection*, television, 1976

Opposite: Rehearsing with Natalie Wood for *Cat on a Hot Tin Roof*, television, 1976

A couple of years ago he appeared in two huge British television hits. As Lord Marchmain in *Brideshead Revisited* he bided his time until he came to the scenes preceding his death when he exploded with a wonderful personal gaiety, raising the quick memories of Coward, the clipped playing of the twenties, the dash of the old matinée idols. 'When the time comes for my own death,' he said, 'I should be very good at it. I seem to do one rehearsal after another these days.' In *A Voyage Round My Father* he got to perfection the stern, playful, moving, incisive eccentricity of John Mortimer's blind father without ever listing into sentimentality. When he has his breath and a part he wants and the time to prepare it as he wants, he can still stun you so that you wake up and believe in him: even though it has got harder for him, and for us, through the years as our memories and his many roles have encrusted themselves on our pupils so that we see him through wrappings of other times, other characters, other days. Yet his capacity to compel belief remains: even through all that, even through a legend which could have put him in a straitjacket.

While we were making our film he was sometimes ill. On one extremely worrying morning we arrived only to clear out half an hour later as he took a bad turn. He had been through long, arduous and punishing assaults of treatment. There was the thrombosis, there had been the huge spread of cancer, there was that 'uproar in the cells'.

Below: With Jeremy Irons and Anthony Andrews in *Brideshead Revisited*

Above: With John Osborne and Melvyn Bragg, Brighton front, 1982

Yet again and again he warbled like a lark, shone like a star. After the first day's shooting – two three-hour sessions plus all the setting up and sorting out – he had champagne for everyone and, seeing how awkward and shy most of us were in the presence, so to speak, of someone we all admired intensely and feared we had overtaxed that day, he rolled out a barrowload of stories, voices, self-mockery, mimicry, giving them to us with easy generosity. We felt as if we had been given 'going away presents' after a party. He likes a drink, people say.

One day we bowled along to Brighton to do some filming with John Osborne. Olivier announced that he had given up drinking 'forever'. It affected the memory, he said, adversely, and he had taken the odd one, or two, and maybe even sometimes three or could it be four in his time, but all that was in the past. Did we know how bad it was for the memory, the liver, the this thing and he forgot which other thing but it didn't do any good at all? No. Seventy-five was an age to take a grip on yourself, sort a few things out, stop wasting your life with fripperies, with damaging fripperies like drinking.

Osborne was sipping champagne.

'Well,' said Sir Laurence, 'just a glass, just the one mind you, so as not to insult my old friend John Osborne here, can't have him drinking alone, oh – wonderful to be in Brighton again, marvellous thank you, thank you very much, you'd better leave the bottle just in case old Johnny might need another glass, you never know.'

And on we went with this supposed, and genuinely, very sick, worn-out old man – an hour or so later roaring through a splendid, full and sufficiently alcoholic lunch ending up, in his case with two puddings and a final, but final little glass of that bubbly stuff. Out onto the promenade for the interview, parading down it like a guardsman, delighted with Osborne's affectionate wit.

Or we were at a party to which he had been invited. He had come although he was very ill and indeed he was. He sat quieter than quiet, eyes closed some of the time, seemingly willing himself out of the room, out of the company. He was no one and wanted no one to etch a mark on him, wanted to be left to his anonymity like some forest bird seeking the retreat most safely suited to its camouflage.

Yet at that very time he was in training to do King Lear.

'In training' meant the usual combination. He gave himself voice lessons every morning, banging away at the piano, pushing his voice down a note at a time, yelling out the notes with uninhibited force and no tunefulness at all. The object was to extend the vocal range.

Then, the physical exercises. Ill as he had been and could still be, he made himself swim about a quarter of a mile every morning. This would give him the stamina and strengthen his arms. He wanted to be strong enough to carry Cordelia.

And, as at all times when he has taken on one of the great roles and wanted to use every minute of rehearsal time to fullest advantage, he learnt the part in its entirety before the very first read-through. And, as with Othello, as on so many other occasions, word came down, eventually, from Manchester, that the assembled cast had been stricken when, at what they thought was a chummy, first-get-together read-through, Olivier had blazed off his part all guns firing.

I asked him if we could come into the rehearsals, knowing the answer. Even a read-through? Not a chance. That was all too private business. It was there that the hunt was on, the pursuit into himself for that man he could have been, and the building up of the external mask which would tell the naked truth.

We were in the garden of his country place for that last interview. A mild English summer day. He had shown me proudly and expertly around the garden which he had so artfully laid out. He had always enjoyed designing gardens. He pointed out the little paths, the surprise views, the bowers and secluded sunny spots. How would he describe this garden? 'Oh, very vicarage,' he said, 'which is just as it should be.'

EPILOGUE

Opposite: At home, 1982

Right: With Joan Plowright, revisiting Chichester, 1982

If only by being a thousand others could Olivier be fully himself, then that personal compulsion has also been the means of giving millions of people pleasure, terror, delight, awe, feelings of splendour, ripples of fun, other lives by courtesy of his great, great talent. If it is true that the enemy was blankness, that the goad was avoiding boredom, that the fear was his own death forever ready to claim him unless he took a life in his hands and escaped it, then his victories have not only saved his life but enriched ours. I am sure that a score of people would give you a score of characters and all of them would be right. But despite the huge presence of that giddily exceptional gift, he has worked for others, brought up children, cossetted friends, entertained all manner of troops, brought on talent and knocked off unnecessary

lights to save on the electricity bill. Taken all in all we will not . . .

He is fearless or makes himself seem so even though he constantly confesses to being frightened to death. Not only the many feats of physical daring, often crazy. Fearless in his determination. At William Walton's Memorial Service in Westminster Abbey with the music, the fine singing, the large crowd of friends, the sophisticated society of music – Olivier went up into the pulpit, limped up, almost, looking tired and not at all well that day and then, starting softly, growing slowly, rolled out the great speech from *Henry V* which Walton worked on with him, loosed it like a quiverful of arrows to all the corners of the Abbey so that we would thrill, with him, to remember his friend through great language.

When Olivier made *Hamlet*, there were many scenes which had to be cut. 'The rule in editing Shakespeare,' he said, 'is to lift out whole scenes. If you trim here and trim there, all you have left is a lot of loose ends.' This is the first part of a soliloquy he hated leaving out: he did, because the film needed it. But he sorely missed the chance to say it:

Ay, so God buy to you! Now I am alone.
O, what a rogue and peasant slave am I!
Is it not monstrous that this player here,
But in a fiction, in a dream of passion,
Could force his soul so to his own conceit
That from her working all his visage wann'd;
Tears in his eyes, distraction in's aspect,
A broken voice, and his whole function suiting
With forms to his conceit? And all for nothing!
For Hecuba!
What's Hecuba to him or he to Hecuba
That he should weep for her? What would he do,
Had he the motive and the cue for passion
That I have? He would drown the stage with tears,
And cleave the general ear with horrid speech;
Make mad the guilty, and appal the free,
Confound the ignorant, and amaze indeed
The very faculties of eyes and ears . . .

Bon voyage, and thanks.